# The Clark Kent Chronicles

## A Mother's Tale Of Life With Her ADHD And Asperger's Son

### Pamela Fagan Hutchins

The Clark Kent Chronicles

Skipjack Publishing books may be purchased for educational, business, or sales promotional use. For information, please write: Sales, Skipjack Publishing, P.O.B. 31160 Houston, TX 77231.

First U.S. Edition

TheClark Kent Chronicles/by Pamela Fagan Hutchins

ISBN-13: 978-0615633763 (Skipjack Publishing)

Written with love for my very own "Clark Kent," who is worth everything and more.

# Acknowledgments

Huge thanks to my editor Meghan Pinson, who managed to keep my ego intact without sacrificing her editorial integrity. Thanks to Penny Williams and all the other ADHD mommas out there. Thanks of generous proportions to my writing group, without whose encouragement and critiques I would not be publishing this book. Big thanks and big up to "Clark Kent" for (grudgingly) granting me permission to tell our tales. And thanks to the power of infinity to my husband Eric, for his patience and support.

Thanks also to Alex Dumetriscu and Heidi Dorey for fantastic cover art. Photography credits go to Eric and me.

# Other Books by Pamela Fagan Hutchins

*Hot Flashes And Half Ironmans: Middle-aged Endurance Athletics Meets The Hormonally Challenged*, Skipjack Publishing

*How To Screw Up Your Kids: Blended Families, Blendered Style*, Skipjack Publishing

*Love Gone Viral: Couples Who Make You Wanna Puke, And How To Be Part Of One*, Skipjack Publishing.

*Puppalicious And Beyond: Life Outside The Center Of The Universe*, Skipjack Publishing

*Easy To Love, But Hard To Raise* (anthology contributor), DRT Press, edited by Kay Marner and Adrienne Ehlert Batista

*Prevent Workplace Harassment*, Prentice Hall, with the Employment Practices Solutions attorneys

Coming Soon:
*Discovering Katie*, Skipjack Publishing
*Leaving Annalise*, Skipjack Publishing
*Conceding Grace*, Skipjack Publishing
*Going For Kona*, Skipjack Publishing

# Table of Contents

# "MY MOTHER IS RUINING MY LIFE."

I started publishing *The Clark Kent Chronicles* when our real-life ADHD WonderKid[1] was in middle school, absolutely the worst time of his life. I know, I'm a fabulous mother.

At first, I only posted my stories to a private family blog. My actions (and scribblings) did not register on the radar of our "Clark[2]." Actually, not much registered on his radar. One of the hallmarks of his ADHD is his

---

[1] At the time I wrote this book, Clark Kent had survived my parenting to reach his junior year in high school.

[2] Of course, Clark isn't his real name, but we nicknamed him Clark Kent long ago. I used pseudonyms throughout this little tome to protect the innocent, criteria which requires my husband Eric and me to use our real names.

incredible lack of observation skills. This serves him well at times.

I branched out. The *Clark Kent Chronicles* vignettes began to pop up in my Facebook statuses. Clark refused to accept my friend request, so he stayed blissfully ignorant, but other people noticed. The kid who drove me nuts, the kid I wrote funny stories about to keep from crying over, delighted my friends.

So I branched further out. By now, I had a public website with a modest following. I expanded my vignettes into essays. Readers loved him. And in a moment of soul-baring self-therapy, I pushed "Confessions of a Guilt-Stricken Mom: Loving My ADHD Son" out into the great unseen masses on the internet.

The response overwhelmed me. My maternal suffering and my attempts to laugh about it touched a nerve. Clark was the boy other stressed-out ADHD parents could read about to feel better about their own kids and themselves. He made it all OK for a lot of people who really were at the end of their endurance. Those parents were learning, like me, that no one had a one-size-fits-all-solution or perfect answer for them: not psychiatrists, psychologists, in-laws, PTA buddies, or strangers in line at Walmart. They were parenting their kids by trial and error, too, and managing, just barely, to survive it.

By this point, Clark had relented and let me into his Facebook world, although I wasn't allowed to interact with him. Too embarrassing. (Kids!) Tentatively, I prodded him to see if he had noticed the *Clark Kent Chronicles* posts in his News Feed.

"Did you see I mentioned you on my blog? It was on Facebook," I asked.

"Uhhhhh," Clark said. Or didn't say, rather.

"I just want to be sure you're OK with me writing about you."

"What?"

I clicked and opened the post "Lacrosse Gloves Make Sense to Me."

"See?"

Clark read. He smiled, then frowned. "Do you have to do this? People will know it's me."

"Like I'm friends with your friends. No one knows your real first name. Plus, our last names are different."

"OK, I guess."

From this exchange, I intuited that he was crazy in love with me writing about him, and that he wanted me to rock on. *Go, Mom, go!* I'm highly empathic like that.

I launched a Facebook fan page. A budding writer himself, Clark became more interested in my writing overall. I wrote a novel, *Going for Kona*, based partly on my feelings about my awesome husband and partly on my feelings about my awesome son. At first, he devoured it. Then he came to *bad parts*, where Mom and Son fought, and Husband died. Big tears ran down his cheeks. He paced circles around the house in his worn-to-a-nub flip-flops. He argued with me to change it. I wouldn't. And he refused to read another word, unable to deal with his enormous middle-school-boy emotions.

But he was proud of me. He started to read my other pieces. Sort of. For a while. Mostly he just daydreamed about his mother becoming the next Great American Author, when he wasn't playing computer games on the sly or hiding his school progress report.

Unfortunately, it was during this time period that *The Clark Kent Chronicles* as a body of work finally broke through his haze and into his cerebral cortex. We had a serious sit-down.

Clark pointed at a sentence in a piece called "Poo Poo on You." "That's not what happened," he said.

"What? It's pretty much what happened. If I wrote exactly what happened I would bore people with 500,000-word manifestos. It's not a lie. I write semi-true. Isn't that better, anyway? You have plausible deniability. You can tell people that your mother just makes this stuff up," I said.

"But not everybody will know that."

"The people that know you know what's true."

He thought about it. He suggested I use a different name for him. I considered it for a couple of seconds. I suggested I continue to use Clark Kent. He relented. Sort of.

"Just don't embarrass me, Mom. You could ruin my life, you know."

"I promise, son, I won't."

A few years passed, and here we are.

Clark, I promise, this isn't going to ruin your life. And if I make any money at all off *The Clark Kent Chronicles*, the first thing I'll do with it is pay for your therapy. I promise.

# WHERE IT ALL BEGAN: LACROSSE GLOVES MAKE SENSE TO ME

My son has ADHD. He is also a near-genius, hilarious, dearly loved, and the most well-adjusted member of our family. When I think of Clark, I see Niagara Falls. I smell pine trees and clear mountain air. I hear Natalie Merchant sing "Wonder."

Clark is special. We always knew he had unique traits (don't we all?), but we fought the ADHD label and diagnosis for many years. Instead, we would empathize with each other that he was disorganized, "his father's child," "out to lunch," and "his own self."

Type A, slightly OCD woman that I am, I just believed I could engineer a solution, that my will and need for control were stronger than anything God and Clark's genetics could put in front of me. We employed every

suggestion we could find to help him, short of medication, until he was in his teens. But no matter what we
did, Clark was still the kid who would leave the kitchen
with an assignment to put up his folded laundry and
forget it by the time he reached the living room, then
happily return to the kitchen after a few meandering laps
around our house to sit down and read *The Ranger's
Apprentice*, without understanding why his mother's face
had just turned purple.

I want to introduce you to this amazing creature, my
son.

In eighth grade, Clark received a commendation in all
four of the standardized TAKS (Texas Assessment of
Knowledge and Skills) subjects. He participated in band
and lacrosse. He played a primary role in his middle
school play, *The Naked King*. And yet he almost drove his
parents crazy with constant, inexplicable Clarkisms along
the way.

Back then, his counselor asked us to teach Clark responsibility for his own actions using Love and Logic
Parenting[3] in conjunction with the assistance we all gave
him on organizational skills. The *staggering* amount of

[3] Techniques to help parents have more fun and less stress
while raising responsible kids of all ages, from the Love and
Logic Institute. http://www.loveandlogic.com/.

assistance we gave Clark with organizational skills, which he absolutely hated, whether it came from the counselor or from us. But the counselor claimed great success with the Love and Logic methodology.

We were supposed to clearly state to Clark that he is responsible for a certain behavior (i.e., turning in completed homework) and that if he chooses not to do the behavior, he is choosing the consequence that goes with it (i.e., yard work).

Logical, right?

Loving, too?

Sure . . . but it didn't work on Clark *at all*. Not a single bit.

It worked amazingly well with his non-ADHD siblings, though, so it was not a total waste. To give you just a taste, I offer up this very one-sided Instant Message conversation between my husband (stepdad) and me (mom). This exchange is about yard work Clark was supposed to do as a consequence for not turning in completed homework.

mom 4:39pm: i told him to go outside and start the yard work/mow at 4:10. then i took a long shower
mom 4:39pm: i started getting ready in the bathroom
mom 4:39pm: at 4:33 i heard noises in the kitchen
mom 4:39pm: it was clark
mom 4:40pm: *"getting a snack"*

mom 4:40pm: i said go back outside you should have done the snack before you started the yard work

mom 4:40pm: he said no, i haven't gotten started out in the yard yet

mom 4:40pm: i said impossible, no snack takes 22 min

mom 4:40pm: he said he made a sandwich

mom 4:40pm: i said that doesn't take 22 minutes, 22 minutes is a 3 course meal

mom 4:40pm: he then said he'd go *right outside*

mom 4:40pm: but he came right back in and said he had no gas so he was going to pull weeds instead of mow. i said ok. he asked me to show him which plants are weeds so i did

mom 4:41pm: he came back in 1 minute later and said there are thorns

mom 4:41pm: i said get gloves if you are concerned about thorns (as you know there were barely any stickers on those plants and no thorns)

mom 4:41pm: he went looking for gloves

mom 4:41pm: couldn't find any (he said)

mom 4:41pm: he went back outside WITH HIS GIANT LACROSSE GLOVES ON, with the fingers that have the size and flexibility of Polish sausage

mom 4:41pm: at this point, i became frustrated

mom 4:41pm: i told him to get the gloves off and get outside mom 4:41pm: i explained to him that it was 4:36 and that we were leaving at 6:30 for his sister's concert and that I was dropping him at his dad's

mom 4:41pm: because he had at least 2 hours of work to do in the yard as he had known since *last night*

mom 4:42pm: and he couldn't go to the concert without a shower, but there wouldn't be time for him to shower because he had to finish

mom 4:42pm: and that after this i couldn't trust him to stay at home alone and do the yard work without supervision, so he had to go to his dad's

mom 4:42pm: AND this was after a very difficult 5 minute conversation trying to get a straight answer out of him about his grades and what his teachers said about any need for extra credit in his classes given all the homework he hadn't turned in

mom 4:42pm: i had to stop him over and over when he would say something nonresponsive designed to make me think he had actually talked to the teacher, and i'd say, that's not what the teacher said, what did the teacher say, and it turned out he hadn't talked to the teachers at all!

mom 4:42pm: so then he started crying because he wasn't going to get to go to the concert

mom 4:43pm: and i only yelled one time, which is a miracle at this point

mom 4:43pm: and i said stop with the tears, this was your choice to waste 40 min, i told you that we had things to do that you might not get to do if you didn't get finished so maybe you'll learn from this but if you don't it will be the same tomorrow

mom 4:43pm: but either way, get outside and get going on the yard work

stepdad 4:44pm: i am still here, take a breath

stepdad 4:44 pm: LACROSSE GLOVES? :-) you have got to admit, that is pretty funny . . .

mom 4:45 pm: ask me tomorrow and maybe it will be funny then . . .

mom 4:47 pm: ok i admit it, it's funny

Besides a lack of organizational skills, another hallmark of the neuro-atypical[4] mind is creative problem-solving. Solutions that don't seem logical to the rest of us, necessarily, but make perfect sense to the child. Clark gives us lots of examples of this trait, sometimes in a dangerous way. Let's just say you don't want to send

---

[4] For purposes of this book, neuro-atypical will describe people on the autism or ADHD spectrums. Conversely, I will use neuro-typical to describe people that have neurological development and states consistent with what most people would think of as normal, particularly with their executive functions and their ability to process linguistic information and social cues.

him out with any type of cutting implement without a clear set of instructions, a demonstration, a run-through, and constant oversight. Which begs the question: Why the heck don't I just do this job myself, if he isn't learning anything from it?

*Ah, but he is, Grasshopper. We must be patient. Very, very patient,* my inner kung fu master says.

(Hold me.)

Note that it truly is a miracle that Clark survives his mother; yelling only once in this lengthy exchange was quite an achievement for me. Intellectually, I know yelling does no good, except to occasionally keep my head from exploding off the top of my neck.

Our learning from the scenario above? That Love and Logic doesn't overcome the wiring of an ADHD brain. Some behaviors just aren't choices for Clark. Some are, though, and one of our challenges is to keep him from gaming our system by using ADHD as an excuse for bad choices, especially as he becomes more parent-savvy.

Lacrosse gloves . . . it *was* pretty funny.

# CONFESSION TIME

The yoke of parental guilt weighs heavy upon me.
Flash back to kindergarten, day two.

School: Your son is reading the Harry Potter books.
He's quite a bit ahead of the other students.

Clark's father Edward and me, proudly: Yes, he loves
to read. He reads aloud to us at bedtime now.

School: We don't think we can keep him interested
and engaged in the kindergarten curriculum. We're
afraid that school will become a negative experience for
him, especially if in his boredom he causes a distraction
for the other students.

Us: [blank stares] Huh?

School: We'd like you to consider moving him direct-
ly to first grade. The teachers will work with him to make
sure he doesn't miss any building blocks.

Us: He's our first child. We had wanted him to be at least as old as his classmates. He seems a bit immature to us. You are the ones with all the experience in education, though. If you really think so . . .

Clark attended a school with only five hundred kids from pre-K through twelfth grade, which seemed an ideal environment, if there was one, in which to skip a grade. We fretted about the impact it might have later. Would he be physically and emotionally mature enough in middle school? What impact would this have on him long-term? But ultimately, we moved him forward.

As a result of this momentous decision, our son, who would have been almost the oldest in his grade, became the youngest. Out of an abundance of caution, I scaled back on my work as a human resources consultant and attorney and volunteered in his classroom two days a week.

First grade didn't go so badly, but we began to notice differences between Clark and the other kids, which we hadn't seen before he started school.

Clark moved 2-3 appendages at all times, although he did not leave his seat and usually did not disrupt others

- He was easily put off-task

- He seemed more disorganized than the other kids
- He had a lot of trouble following sequences of instructions
- He either did not remember or did not tell the truth about homework, although we were able to double-check his assignments against the reminders sent home by the teacher.

In short, Clark displayed behavior that was quite similar to that of other first-grade boys, yet more pronounced. We called this type of behavior acting "lunchy" in our family — short for "out to lunch." Clark's dad was the king of lunchiness, and Clark came by his traits in a genetically and possibly even environmentally predictable manner.

Had Clark not been our first child, we might have noticed his other developmental differences earlier and more readily. He had some odd mannerisms. For instance, he frequently (constantly?) waggled his left hand and ran in circles to the left. In some of my more honest and middle-of-the-night terror types of moments, I wondered if he was autistic. But we didn't have experience or other children to compare him to, so he was simply our son. Quick annual visits to his pediatrician revealed nothing more than a needle phobia. No one else thought he was anything but cute—or if they did, they didn't share it with us, even my physician father (or my mother, who after reading these words when I first published them, confessed she had suspected autism as well). We looked for the ways in which Clark was normal, not the ways in which he was not.

First grade became second. Clark's difficulties became more pronounced. From a sheer brainpower and creativity perspective, he soared. But he now regularly lied to us about schoolwork and chores. Still, everyone kept giving him a thumbs-up. I wondered where I was failing as a parent that he was so untruthful, but I was reassured by, again, a pediatrician, that lying was an expected developmental stage, and age-appropriate.

*Pat, pat. There, there, worrywart mom. Everything is going to be all right.*

Second grade became third. Boy, we were really struggling now. And we had his younger sister Susanne to compare to him. The differences between their first grade experiences were stark, Rainman to Charlie Babbitt. Could it just be gender?

Clark's wonderful third grade teacher at his small private school in the U.S. Virgin Islands reassured me, "Clark will be fine. He'll have a fabulous secretary some day and run rings around all of us."

Third grade became fourth. Another wonderful teacher. She promised me Clark was an angel, brilliant, and well worth her minor additional efforts. She noted that all she had to do to keep Clark with her was pass by him in the aisle as she commenced speaking, gently touch him on the shoulder and say his name.

At home, meanwhile, we were strategizing daily on how to motivate him to tell the truth and do his assignments in and out of class. We tried positive incentives. Praise. Rewards. Gold stars.

Nothing worked.

We tried punishments, like revocation of privileges and grounding. What a joke. I can say with confidence that punishments did not work at all on my son. They felt like arbitrary exercises.

We tried prayer. I cried and I worried. Sound familiar?

And then we came to fifth grade.

# THE GUILT STARTS HERE

Ah, fifth grade. Hellish, horrible fifth grade. Up until now, compassionate teachers had smoothed our path, teachers who loved their students and wanted the best for them. In fifth grade, we were not so lucky.

I have blacked out most of this year from my memory banks. I don't want to remember, because I feel too guilty for not saving him from it. Clark seems to have blacked it out as well—even to have done so at the time. However, he became noticeably more anxious and down over the course of the year.

One event sums it up for me, the culmination of the ineffective and unjust punishments and belittling comments about and to Clark and us. It is important to note that Clark's experience matched that of other "neuro-typical" (a descriptive term I did not learn until much later) students that year and the one previous; the complaints about this teacher were coming from increasingly angry parents.

Here's what happened. The teacher, let's call her Ms. X, was administering a test to the class. One of Clark's challenges then was that if he became immersed in a book, he would not re-emerge without physical stimuli. He loved his fantasy world of books. The only thing he loved more than fantasy was the computer, which we had already learned was a dangerously addictive space for him and a pastime we had to limit carefully. In fact, if he had too much game time, he would become angry and hostile — even physical — when we pulled him away; he would "game" to the exclusion of all other life activities, even at the tender age of ten. The child had spent most of his years on earth grounded from screens, sometimes for months at a time. The issue at school, though, was books, which had a similar although slightly less dramatic effect on him.

Back to Ms. X and the test. Ms. X had taught Clark for six months by this time, and she knew him well. We had talked to her about Clark from day one, and his previous teachers had told her how to help Clark succeed. She found him to be too much trouble, though; she had let us know in no uncertain terms during our mid-year parent-teacher conference that he was "impossible" and "took too much of her attention away from the other students," although she could give us no examples of how.

On this day (all parties agreed), Clark sat at his desk reading a book until the bell rang to start the day. Ms. X passed out the test and gave instructions. Standing beside her desk at the front of the room, she told the students to start the test.

At the far back side of the room, Clark didn't break free from what he was reading. He was in another world. Not, in my opinion, based on my vast, frustrated experience with my son, maliciously or rebelliously so—just joyously, exasperatingly so. He was on a journey into fantasy, and he would not be able to return on his own. While the class took the test for twenty-five minutes, he flew at forty thousand feet above Hogwarts with Harry, Ron, and Hermione. And Ms. X sat silently and watched him, ignoring the coaching she had received on how to get his focus to return to the class. She sat there and did nothing.

When she called time, she passed by Clark, took his blank paper, and chastised him loudly in front of the other students for not taking the test. She kept him in at recess as a punishment.

I don't know about the rest of you parents of neuro-atypical children out there, or even parents of neuro-typical kids, but the bad faith and casual cruelty in her passive-aggressive actions still take my breath away five years later. This woman, this teacher of my child, this person entrusted with the gift of contributing to his development, this twenty-year veteran of fifth-grade teaching, this THING who knew from us, from Clark and from the other teachers and administrators at his school that all Clark needed in the way of accommodation was a gentle touch on the shoulder and a reminder to return to planet Earth just sat there, watched him, and did nothing, then embarrassed and punished him. She knew he wasn't making a choice. Yet she treated him as if he had. [Insert expletives and choice names here.]

So, up to the school I sped the next morning after reviewing the contents of my ten-year-old son's backpack with him and hearing his explanation of the blank test with a big zero on top. I can guarantee you I made an impression that day, although I cringe to think what it was. The end result was that, for the first time, these experienced educators suggested we test Clark for ADHD. And I let them know that if anyone in their school ever treated my son like Ms. X had again, I would pull my private school[5] tuition and take him elsewhere,

---

[5] At the time, I didn't even know I had an ADHD child, much less did I know about required public school accommodations, discussed later in this book. However, even if I

no matter what the tests said. They apologized profusely, excused Ms. X for having exceptionally trying personal circumstances (like I cared, at that point) and promised to look into it.

And so, for the first time, we tested.

And the testing psychologist said, "Well, hmmm, I'm not sure, he's certainly not a severe case if he is ADHD, yeah, ummm, well, it's your decision, but I'm loathe to label him, especially if the school will have these records. How about I counsel him on organizational skills and keep an eye on the situation? I'll prepare an instruction manual for teachers on how to accommodate him, and you can share it with the school? If you want a referral to a psychiatrist for medications, I could give you one, but I'm not sure he needs them."

Edward (Clark's dad): "Well, Clark reminds me of me, and I turned out all right. He just has trouble getting motivated. Drugs have too many side effects. We'll work with him, too."

Me: "I guess . . ."

If doubts had plagued me before, they tortured me like a prison of war. My (now) ex-husband's maddening behaviors and stories about his childhood suddenly

---

had known these things, private schools are not required to provide accommodations.

made sense. And Clark was a carbon copy of his father, except that he was ten times worse, according to his paternal grandmother.

But if my ex was undiagnosed with ADHD, he had still made it through sans drugs. He was convinced Clark could, too. We read mounds of paper and scoured the interwebs on ADHD, we sought out support groups and counseling for ourselves, but nothing answered the question of what we were to do. We were at a loss.

# There Once Was a Man From Nantucket

And now, for comic relief, a demonstration of why I write prose rather than poetry: Odes to my husband and three youngest kids, in limerick style. I framed these for them one Christmas. They were not impressed.

**1. Liz "Bean"**: Our high school swimming teenager with more clothes, shoes, makeup, and hair straighteners than the rest of us put together.

There once was a girl from Bellaire
Who daily did straighten her hair
A fast-swimming teen
A Facebooking Bean
She can never decide what to wear

**2. Clark**: The Dallas Cowboys' biggest fan. I couldn't limit myself to just one verse here.

> There lives here a boy named Clark
> He treats school much like a lark
> If he ever gets through
> What he's started to do
> We are sure he will leave quite a mark

> A dramatic and unruffled soul
> A haircut a lot like a bowl
> Witten's best fan
> Homework not in his plan
> To be a big dork is his goal

**3. Susanne**: Our middle schooler whose hygiene habits indicate she is not yet interested in boys. Her loves are dogs, swimming, and disagreeing.

> Susanne Marie is her name
> Contrariness is her main game
> She's strong and she's tall
> She likes dogs best of all
> But her showering skills are quite lame

**4. Eric**: And then there is my long-suffering island-boy-turned-Texas-redneck wannabe-triathlete husband, who puts up with me posting his most embarrassing moments on my blog, *Road to Joy*.

> There once was a man from St. Croix
> With a fanny as fine as a boy's
> I may give him heck
> But I love his red neck
> He inspires the name *Road to Joy*

# "THANKS, DAD."

Clark had ADHD whether we were ready to admit it or not. Before too many years passed, we had embraced the concept and were working within the diagnosis. But the diagnosis itself begged a few questions. Mainly, what is ADHD, why does my kid have to have it, and what can we do about it?

In order to understand what ADHD is, it first important to understand what it isn't. ADHD is not a made-up excuse for failing to turn in an occasional homework assignment, nor is it a self-serving justification to take performance-enhancing drugs[6]. ADHD is not an illness

---

[6] Most ADHD kids hate taking meds. Yet the secondary market for ADHD meds with the college-age crowd is stunning. In a non-ADHD person, the meds have a tremendous sharpening effect. On ADHDers like our teenage Clark,

or a temporary condition. It is not autism, nor is it a brain injury, and it is not a weakness of will.

ADHD is a permanent disorder (God, I hate that word) of the brain. It is a neurological difference in the way the brain functions, as compared to the neuro-typical rest of us, a difference characterized by inattention and distractibility, impulsivity, and hyperactivity. We see these traits and others daily in Clark. I will delve into the others later.

Dr. Martin L. Kutscher describes it way better than I can in his book *The ADHD E-book: Living As If There Is No Tomorrow*. He says:

> The chief difficulty is that people with ADHD cannot inhibit the present moment long enough to consider the future. ADHD behaviors make sense once we realize that they are based on reactions that take only the present moment into account. It is not that Johnny doesn't *care* about the future; it is that the future and the past do not even exist. Such is the nature of the disability. If you want to make sense of inexplicable behaviors out of someone with ADHD, just ask yourself: "What behavior makes sense if you had only four seconds left to live?" For example, if you only had four seconds left to live, it would make sense

the meds barely bring him up to functioning in the non-ADHD world.

to play videogames instead of do homework. After all, why do homework if college doesn't exist?[7]

Oh my, and Dr. Kutscher has never even met Clark! Clark earned the moniker *Clark Kent the WonderKid* by exemplifying this four-seconds-left-to-live model. In Clark's mind, it's not possible to get run over by a car if he runs out into the street without looking. There's no way he'll chop his fingers off if he grips the knife around the blade. He really can leap tall buildings in a single bound, as long as he doesn't have to move past dreaming about it to doing it. *No future* means complete invincibility and complete capability. Meet *The WonderKid* — and his mostly flummoxed, frequently tired parents. *Clark Kent* fits, too. In his mind, Clark is Superman, but to the rest of us, he's bumbling, awkward Clark Kent.

It's not all billowing red capes and saving the world, however. As if the core characteristics of ADHD weren't tough enough, it also comes with emotionalism, quick anger, lying, and a bunch of other difficult behaviors. It is estimated that 49% of ADHD children exhibit the behavior of chronic lying, as compared to 5% of "typical" children. Clark falls squarely into that first group —

---

[7] The ADHD E-Book: Living as if There is No Tomorrow, Dr. Martin L. Kutscher, 2002, p. 3-4.

although he is lying less frequently as he gets closer to adulthood.

Dr. Kutscher, bless his heart, has written many other articles and books on pediatric neurology, so I turn to him again to explain how the ADHD spectrum can look similar to the autistic disorders spectrum (which includes autism and Asperger's Syndrome), yet is not the same.

ADHDers typically have trouble with "Executive Functions," with subsequent difficulties in their relationship with others. Usually, though, they have adequate capacity for empathy—but may have trouble inhibiting their behavior long enough to show it. Conversely, many children with Autistic Spectrum may appear to have a short attention span, but just aren't able to stay focused on situations they don't understand.

It is probably best to consider ADHD as sometimes sharing the following symptoms with—but not being part of—the Autistic Disorders Spectrum:

· *Poor reading of social cues* (Johnny, you're such a social klutz. Can't you see that the other children think that's weird?)

· *Poor ability to utilize self-talk to work through a problem* (Johnny, what were you thinking?! Did you ever think this through?)

· *Poor sense of self-awareness* (Johnny's true answer to the above question is probably "I don't have a clue. I guess I wasn't actually thinking.")

· *Do better with predictable routines*

· *Poor generalization of rules* (Johnny, I told you to shake hands with your teachers. Why didn't you shake hands with the *principal*?)[8]

I don't know about you guys, but I'm almost worn out just thinking about it. And if *we're* tired, imagine how exhausting it is for these ADHD kids whose minds, and often bodies, are lit up with a couple of simultaneous pinball games. Don't worry, though. We're almost done. There's one last point I need expert support on, so hang with me a little longer.

Many kids with ADHD have what are called co-morbid conditions, such as learning disabilities, oppositional defiance disorder, anxiety, depression, Asperger's Syndrome, and many more. Dr. Kutscher explains that there are a myriad of co-morbid disorders that exist with the patient or within the family[9], such as with an ADHD parent. We have recently learned, for example, that Clark

---

8 Autism Spectrum Disorders: Sorting it Out, Dr. Martin L. Kutscher, 2004, 2006 (copied exactly as Dr. Kutscher wrote it).

9 The ADHD E-Book: Living as if There is No Tomorrow, Dr. Martin L. Kutscher, 2002, p. 13.

has a high-functioning level of Asperger's Syndrome. This helps explain his perseverating[10] behaviors, encyclopedic thinking, concrete thinking, oversensitivity to certain stimuli, and unusual movements, among other behaviors.

Which brings us to the "Why does my kid have to have it?" question. Theories abound. They include brain injuries in utero and exposure to pesticides, but the experts usually point to genetics. Heredity is the most common factor in the occurrence of ADHD in children; kids with ADHD often have parents with neuropsychiatric conditions of their own. Clark's dad, Edward, has ADHD and co-morbid anxiety. *Thanks, Dad!*

Families are inherently complicated, but they get even more so when ADHD is involved. The entire family is buffeted by the stress of ADHD; goodness knows our family feels like we share Clark's ADHD. I love my son madly, but I ain't gonna lie, he adds more stress to my life than the four other kids combined.

The most important thing that does not cause ADHD (and pay attention here, because this is the heartbreak

---

[10] The persistence of a repetitive response after the cause of the response has been removed, or the response continues to different stimuli.

and pet peeve of every parent of an ADHD child on the planet): BAD PARENTING.

So there.

Finally, the hardest question of all: what (do I think you) can you do about ADHD? Well, gosh, that's a question that will take the rest of this book for me to answer. But I can give you the Cliff Notes version: there are lots of things you can try that will help some people, but not everyone. The longer version: I have learned slowly and oh-so-painfully over the years that no one has all the answers for the parents of kids with ADHD. We pull valuable pieces of information from everywhere possible and assemble and reassemble them until we get the best fit possible for our kids. You won't find me trying to push a particular answer on you.

What I've learned, and what I hope to pass on to you, is to look for the joy and to be patient and flexible as possible.

# WHAT LOVE CAN DO

A few years ago on August 28th, I made a decision that changed my life.

For the better. Forever.

All those years ago and one day ago, I drank alone for the last time. All those years and one day ago, I drank *too much*, alone, and damaged my relationships and myself for the last time.

The catalyst? My son, Clark Kent, the ADHD WonderKid, at the age of eight, told his teacher that he was worried about his mother.

Now, see, I've gone and made myself cry already when I'd barely started writing this story! Sheesh. I hate it when I do that.

Anyway, Clark's words stopped me cold. I knew what he meant. I knew I drank too many Bloody Marys and too often, and that it had started years and years before. I knew my face had puffed up, that I woke up hungover over-frequently, that I cut out of work early to drink wine with my girlfriends, that I acted awful when I was drunk, that I no longer exercised. I knew that a hungover me lacked the bandwidth to deal effectively with my kids' issues, let alone Clark's distressing behaviors and challenges. I knew that and a lot more.

But all that was about me, and I didn't care enough about me to do anything about it. I tried, sure, I tried cutting back any number of times. For all the good it did. But for Clark or my other kids, I would do almost anything.

So I told my boss I would see him in ten days. He didn't ask why, which said a lot. I boarded a plane for St. Lucia and I checked into a mind and body spa. I planned a week of rejuvenation while I dried out. I'm not a joiner; I wish I was, but I'm not. AA was not for me. So, St. Lucia, solo.

So what did I really do when I got there?

Got drunk by myself in a panicked, sobbing frenzy on night one on anything and everything I could find in the mini-bar. So drunk that I woke up the next morning and didn't remember falling asleep in the bathtub with the TV on. *Congratulations, Pamela. You go, girl.*

I didn't think I could get lower than I had been after I heard Clark's words from his teacher's mouth, but I did. The morning after the last time I drank alcohol was the lowest point of my life, even beating out my later divorce, the bloody aftermath, and the custody battle that ensued. I despised myself. Not for the first time, I wished I were selfish enough to kill myself. It seemed like that would be so much easier.

For me.

But this was not about me. It was about my kids.

So, I picked myself up and put on my too-tight stretchy exercise clothes that used to fit and marched with gritted teeth up 7,000 steps in the heat to the mind and body center. I spent the remaining six days (instead of the planned seven) alone in my mind. My version of Elizabeth Gilbert's year of eating, praying, and loving, I guess. I sweated. I cried. I replayed Clark's words and my failures over and over in my mind. I felt like absolute crap. I walked the beaches until my feet were as smooth as a baby's bottom. And then I came home dry.

It was hard. So very, very hard.

My husband drank quite a lot at the time, and he didn't slow down for me. The bad marriage I had drowned in booze was impossible to tolerate without anesthetic and contributed to my urge to drink. Most of my friends were heavy drinkers, too, and they viewed my decision to stop drinking as a personal indictment of their choices.

Who was this about, anyway?

Right. My kids. I kept going.

I counted the days out painfully, one by one. I again rejected the idea of AA, not only because of my anti-joiner bent, but out of fear of the impact it would have on my high-profile career in our small community. I did it alone, with only one real friend who was aware and still with me *(thanks, Nat!)*, in the middle of the Cruzan-rum-rich island environment of St. Croix, USVI.

Years later, three months had passed. Alcohol absti-nence started getting easier — not a lot easier, but easier. And I felt better, I looked better. I lost weight. I acted nicer. I became more energetic and productive, crisper. I started running again.

And Clark quit worrying about me. (Tiny little sob again, but I've got it under control now, no worries.)

I am now married to a man who gave up alcohol on our first date. The same date on which he told me I stopped his heart. Eric wasted (pardon the pun) no time in showing me he meant to be my hero, and he is, for more by far than putting up with me writing about his Ironman underwear. *(Woops, sorry, honey.)*

People ask me how I do it all. I don't know. But I do know that a drunken Pamela could not have run five marathons and written two novels in one year while parenting and holding down a day job, even with the world's greatest husband.

And it's not just productivity that the alcohol drained away from me. I have more money for what I need to do as well. I refuse to tally how much I've saved by cutting out booze—it would be too depressing. But I am so grateful that when hard times came to our household and I needed to watch every penny, I wasn't battling myself for alcohol money to spend on wine at World Market.

I know alcohol doesn't affect most people the way it does me. Most people can drink in moderation and still thrive, achieve, and parent. I am happy for them, and envious. My non-drinking is not a judgment of what I think others should do, it is what I must do.

I'd love to say that after this many years dry that I never think about drinking, but that is not true. Sometimes I wake up with the sweats, dreaming that I have fallen off the wagon. In those dark moments in the middle of the night, I long to search the house for a bottle of comfort. Every time I travel, the urge strikes, because I used to drink alone in hotel rooms. Now, instead, I sit awake all night, writing to distract myself and praying for the day I never travel alone again.

I don't want to waste another day or night of my life. I want to be the best me I can be 24/7, for my kids, my husband, and finally, for myself. I know only one way to do this, so I will stay true. One day at a time. One year at a time. For the rest of my life.

Thank you, Clark.

# AND FOR OUR NEXT TRICK, WE'LLL BLEND.

Summer vacation spots, Thanksgiving dinner menus, birthday breakfasts, rabid devotion to Texas A&M football . . . culture . . . tradition . . . family . . . it's great stuff at our house.

Family culture evolves slowly, but becomes so ingrained in us that even though we take it for granted most of the time, we will go to battle over it in a heartbeat. It is who we are. What happens, though, when family structure changes? What survives, what dies, what is reborn? When Eric and I decided to get married, we spent a lot of time considering this. Because there's everyone else's perfect little families, and then there's our almost-a-Brady-Bunch: Eric, me, three of his, and two of mine.

Eric and I faced a restructuring challenge when his youngest daughter Liz (13 at the time) moved in with

Eric and me, Clark (11) and Susanne (9). We had been navigating the "stepsiblings living in separate houses" issue, and, while that was not without its own perils, the boats had been sailing on relatively smooth waters. As smooth as possible, at least, considering Eric's bumpy introduction to ADHD parenting. Our main issue until the blend event was hurt feelings over the time each parent spent with non-birth kids.

And then we blended—with a plan. I believe anything that needs doing should be done with a plan. And a schedule. Preceded by research. (My husband actually puts up with this Type-A nonsense. Can you imagine the special hell that I am to my ADHD son?)

We had just moved to Houston from the Virgin Islands, so we had three kids with no friends yet newly thrown together in the house for a long summer of empty days with me—I work from home—to shepherd them. Me, who was *trying* to work while Clark chanted, "I like cheese" and circled the nearly-bare rooms all day.

Clark was what you might call change-resistant, and the move was harder on him than anyone else. Oh yeah, and we were broke. Zero cash, flat-out broke. We weren't going to be able to throw money at this problem.

Our blending plan/schedule involved holding themed family events each night of the week, on the cheap. Monday, ping-pong. Tuesday, board games.

Wednesday, movies. Thursday, kids cook. Friday, swim night. Saturday, go out (on a strict budget). We had a rotation for which kid got to choose which movie, which board game, the menu, what our night out would be. A rotation that Clark never quite grasped, despite the color-coded chart on the wall. He was always wondering who and what were next. But the rest of us got the hang of it, and we kept it up all summer. Some vestiges remain even now.

It was powerfully effective. Why?

Because we did things as a family. We did not sit around and whine about what to do; we were active. We established a pattern that the kids looked forward to repeating. We honored each other's choices, although we weren't above bartering with Clark to try to get out of another game of Risk.

By August, we decided our fledgling relationships were ready to leave the nest; we attempted a two-week cross-country journey from Houston to Maine and back with the five of us in the Suburban on an impossibly tight budget. We toted an ice chest full of turkey, bread, mayo and soft drinks. We listened to audiobooks from the public library. We logged five thousand miles without killing Clark. It was a triumph!

And on that trip, we created our own memories as a new family. On each of the next thirteen days, we stopped at every state line (twenty-eight in all) and took a photo; Eric and I alternated as photographer, and Lenny our pet armadillo appeared in every picture. If someone was asleep, we woke their lazy butt up and dragged them out of the Suburban anyway. We visited Eric's oldest daughter Marie at her university apartment. Liz kept a trip journal and made a scrapbook in which she dutifully logged every odd thing Clark said along the way. There were a lot of them.

If you had asked me at the age of twenty-two whether I wanted a failed first marriage, an ADHD/Asperger's child, and the responsibility for blending a family in my final marriage, I would have cringed and said, "Not just no, but hell no!" But I would not trade any of our five kids, who are beautiful and perfect in part because of who their parents are, nor would I trade the opportunity to have them all in my life just to have skipped the hard parts. I wouldn't want to miss out on the incredible journey that Eric and I travel together, blending the worlds and traditions of these young people until that wonderful moment when we hear all of them yelling at each other without respect to bloodlines, and we can say to each other, "Ah, at last, we've done it. Everything is just perfect."

*"Now quit yelling at your stepsister — and stay on your own side of the back seat!"*

# POO POO ON YOU

On Sundays, Eric and I assign chores to the kids. If they get the minimum done, they stay in our good graces. If they contribute more than the minimum at a level appropriate to their age and maturity, they get an allowance. One Sunday in particular will go down in history.

At age sixteen, Liz reliably kept her eye on the prize and did everything we asked of her with no fuss. Twelve-year-old Susanne made it a challenge, but we could generally cajole her through the process. Both girls are neuro-typical.

Clark, at thirteen, was another story. He had a long history of avoiding unpleasant consequences for his actions by omitting the truth, dodging the questions, and flat-out lying. While he is a charming boy, these are not charming habits. We had tried everything we (and our many counselors) could think of, but nothing got through to him for long.

The Sunday in question was more of the same.

We gave Clark four tasks: clean your room, clean and mop your bathroom, change the cat box and sweep the area around it, and bag and dispose of the (mountains of) dog poo in the backyard. Clark did not have the most pleasurable jobs that week, but we do rotate poo week amongst the kids to keep it fair.

We know that Clark's ADHD makes it difficult for him to do a series of tasks. We're prepared to help him deal with the organizational challenges; we expect to. But his struggle with telling the truth causes us real consternation.

On three of the four tasks, Clark "didn't hear me" ask him to mop, "forgot" to put the cat litter into the empty cat box, "didn't understand" that cleaning up the cat area meant to sweep up cat kibbles in addition to sweeping up cat litter, and "thought his room looked great already."

The kicker was the dog poo.

When we discovered the many issues with Clark's other chores, Eric looked into the trash bin to see if it contained a bag of poo. No bag, no poo. He asked me to check and see if poo cleaning had occurred in the back yard. Surprisingly, it had. The backyard was poo-less.

We asked Clark if he had done the poo clean-up.

His answer? "Yes." Of course.

"Where's the bag of poo, then?" I asked.

"I put it in the trash bin," Clark replied.

"Show us," I said.

"What do you want me to do, dig around in there?"

"Yes."

Wide-open fast-thinking eyes looked back at me, un-blinking; then he shuffled off to locate the poo bag.

He reported his lack of success ten minutes later. Af-ter we confirmed the absence of the poo bag—although Clark smelled like plenty of other unpleasant residue after his dumpster dive—the three of us went around the yard and the house looking for the bag.

"Someone must have taken it, Mom," Clark said.

"Clark, we have not had a real problem with dump-ster theft from our bin, and if we had, why would they take only the bag of poo? No one steals poo, Clark," I said.

"Well, what if it is just *gone*, Mom?"

"Clark, it isn't just gone. It never existed, did it?"

**"Well, I didn't throw it over into the neighbor's yard."**

Both our heads whipped around.

Eric jumped in. "What was that? Someone threw poo in the neighbor's yard? Who? When?"

"It wasn't me, it was like, last summer, and it wasn't me."

Uh oh.

This was the end for Clark. We reminded him of the little boy who cried wolf, and that he had cried wolf one too many times with us. We did not believe there was ever a bag of poo in the bin. Moreover, we were getting out the flashlights and doing a little recon in the neighbors' yards right that second unless he came clean about the poo.

"Wait, guys, wait. How about we look for the poo bag tomorrow? Maybe it's under a bush or something in the back yard," Clark pleaded.

The poo was getting deeper.

I gave a fraction of an inch. "OK, Clark; find this bag of poo after school tomorrow. But know that first thing tomorrow morning, we are going to look in all three neighboring yards in daylight."

The next day didn't go so well for young Clark. A lack of focus is one thing, and some of his incomplete chores I could chalk up at least partially to focus. Lying is another thing altogether, though, and while it's a propensity of kids with ADHD, it's not something we can tolerate. Even if he does blurt out the truth in an unguarded moment.

Thank goodness, he was not (yet) a good liar.

# THAT BOY IS MY HEART.

Oh, the exquisite pain of motherhood. The love so deep that even the thought of something marring our child's perfect life feels like the squeeze of a garlic press to our maternal hearts. We want to give them an easy time in life, to prevent the boo-boos, not just kiss them away. I feel this way for each of my kids. But Clark is special—I can't pretend otherwise. That boy is my heart.

For those of you who are parents of young neuro-atypical kids, some of your most raw moments are yet to come. I don't say that to minimize the challenges you've already faced; there are many tough ones in the early years. But the middle school years, oh my, the middle school years, those are the ones that bring a mama to her knees. Middle school sucks.

I thought it sucked when I was in middle school, and I am not only neuro-typical, but I excelled in almost every way imaginable, so I don't know how it could have been any easier for me. Yet it still sucked.

Every kid at this age goes through so many hormonal changes and self-doubts. Social interactions take on a whole new importance. Peer relationships are everything. Young boys begin to mature physically and emotionally, albeit more slowly than the girls. They become braver, bigger, stronger, and rougher on each other.

My neuro-atypical sweetheart of a son hit middle school like it was the Great Wall of China. His slightly off behaviors—which we, his family, get and love—combined with his random outbursts and apparent emotional insensitivity, pushed his peers away. His inside-out and backwards t-shirts and flip-flops in the dead of winter may not have helped. He had few real relationships outside the family, and our attempts to facilitate interactions with other boys seemed like waterboarding torture after a while.

The insensitivity others saw in Clark is not unusual for a neuro-atypical child. Those subtle cues about the things that are OK and not OK to say and do whiz right past the kids with ADHD or Asperger's Syndrome (Clark's personal co-morbid) or autism. Clark missed those cues just like he missed cues on homework and chores. He said really odd stuff that hurt others' feelings or caused discomfort; but mostly, he said nothing at all.

And it was at this age that Clark's lack of focus immobilized him in the activities he loved best. Clark loves football. He is a serious student of the game, a strategist, a potential coach someday. But *playing* football? Nope. He tried. It was impossible for him in middle school. So was lacrosse. His teammates had developed greater focus and aggression.

Focus? Physical aggression? Ummmm, I don't think so! Not with my ADHD tweener. Clark would find himself in the middle of the action, watching in awe from the best seat in the house. He wasn't unhappy; he just wasn't involved.

And as the other kids became more daring, Clark remained mired in fear and sensitivity. His fears were so large that he couldn't express them; only the size of his pupils let us know he wasn't being stubborn, he was terrified. Roller coasters? Not on your life. Snowboarding? Nope. Skateboarding? Didn't work out so well. Loud 3-D movies? Never. You get the picture. The list is long. All the "boy" stuff.

So what did he want to do? He wanted to retreat into his fantasy world, he wanted to game on the computer. He had "friends" there to play with. He could succeed there, just like he did in his mind. He was the superhero. He was the warrior. Total immersion was his goal.

We kept pulling him out, and pulling him out, and pulling him out. The separation made him angry, sometimes really angry, to the point of shocking physical and emotional meltdowns.

If he couldn't have the computer, he would stay up all night reading fantasy books. Sure, we'd catch him, and turn off the lights several times a night. But he still woke up in a daze the next day, exhausted and even less ready to face the perils of middle school.

We stayed the course with the various treatments our providers recommended, and we made it through. High school was far better than middle school. All those garlic-press clenches on my heart took a few years off my life, though. I shredded, I healed, I shredded again. But I'm a mom; I can take it.

Why do I share this with you all? Because, for one, I think foreknowledge of challenges empowers us to face them. For another, I want you to know from another mom that it does get better. Maturity does help. The symptoms of ADHD do lessen.

New challenges pop up, like, Oh my gosh, how can I ever let this child drive a car? How can I put him and others at risk knowing how many "signals" he misses when the stakes are so much lower? And how can I trust him not to self-medicate with drugs and alcohol, when they may make him feel like all his sharp edges are softly, wonderfully rounded off? How can I keep him from killing himself in some crazy accident I can't even predict when he tries something the rest of us would know was insane, yet seems logical to him?

Ugh.

Yet it is a fact that ADHD kids can grow up into happy and successful people. I know many of them. I hear from many of them. Clark will. Your kids will. Sometimes it will hurt like hell, but you will survive, too. Hang in there. Middle school will come and go. Hug that special child tight and know that one of the blessings God has given him or her is a resilience the likes of which most of us will never know.

# TRUTH OR CONSEQUENCES?

When it comes to raising responsible kids, I am no expert. But Eric and I do have five kids between us. Call us well-practiced, at least. The key principle we live by? Truthfulness. At our house, our kids hear us say super-annoying things like these:

- We would rather hear bad news than no news at all.
- Do you think I would keep my job if I lied to my boss like you lied to me?
- Tell us the truth and we'll reduce the punishment. Lie to us, and we'll find out anyway and raise it.
- If you lied like that to your friends, you'd have no friends.

All of our kids have lied to us about one thing or another. Certainly, young kids go through a phase where lying is common and noncritical, but the stakes rise as they get older.

We reward truth-telling and tackle lying as a "choose to lie, choose the consequences" foul. The worst consequences we can dream up are reserved for lying, and we make sure the kids know about them up front. We tailor the consequences to each child for maximum motivation. Money incentivizes one, so we take away allowance. Socializing is most important to another; no phone calls or playdates. Screens are the pressure point for the third (and I'll bet you can figure out which one). You get the picture.

Our system works fairly well with our neuro-typical children, but not at all with Clark. He believes lying has no consequence because he will never get caught. Clark's grasp of reality is tenuous, and he knows with a moral certainty that he is smarter than anyone on the planet.

In addition to instituting choice/consequences, we have to remain accountable for involved parenting, for structuring rules that motivate the kids to be accountable. When we show up earlier than the kids expect us—or when they don't expect us at all—just once or twice, it works wonders on them. Requiring receipts with change, like an employer would, encourages them to be honest.

Keeping their friends' parents' phone numbers in our mobile phone contacts makes them sit up a little straighter. And friending all their friends on MySpace and Facebook works, too — over time, they forget we're even there.

All bets are off, though, when it comes to lying and the ADHD child. Lying is a symptom of ADHD, part of the "The only time frame is NOW or HUH????" aspect of their brains. When our son takes his meds, his truth-telling shoots up along with his helpfulness around the house. Without the meds . . . his truthfulness flatlines. But Clark didn't start taking medication until he was nearly fourteen and starting his freshman year of high school. Before then, it was not so pretty.

A few weeks before eighth grade let out for summer, Clark got a note from his theater teacher that said he was failing her class because he hadn't turned in an assignment. The note required a parent's signature.

Clark returned the note to his teacher signed "Susie Jackson" — there ain't no Susie Jackson in his family. The theater teacher emailed me to gently inquire/inform.

Woopsie.

Clark earned himself two hours' outdoor labor every day for the entire summer, and zero tolerance on un-truthfulness in any form. Yes, lying is a symptom of ADHD, and we try to guide him with positive reinforcement to be truthful, but handing a forged note to a teacher raised the ante. Unfortunately, only the most present-moment of consequences seem to work, and we soon learned that Clark was not undergoing a radical behavior change under the labor consequence.

Case in point: Eric casually mentioned to me one day that Clark needed to bring Eric's mountain bike home from his father's house, as it had been gone from our house for two weeks since Clark last borrowed it. If you want to be a stickler about it—always a bad place to go with Clark—the problem was serious. We'd forbidden Clark to use Eric's bike *at all* after Clark had left it in the driveway despite repeated instructions to bring it inside. Thieves had already removed Susanne's bicycle from her father's driveway, and he lived in a nice neighborhood. Our cars had been jacked twice in our driveway that year, and our neighborhood was even nicer.

Clark said he didn't take the bicycle. He claimed to have looked for it, and he promised us it wasn't in his dad's garage.

Well, we knew better than to leave it at that.

So we asked Susanne: "When was the last time you saw Eric's bike, and where?"

Susanne innately knows where everything is, partly due to a special sixth sense, partly due to hyperaware-ness, and partly because she is a nosey little devil.

Without hesitation, Susanne said, "Clark rode it over to Dad's."

Hmmmm, Susanne never erred about where things were, and she had no reason to think her answer would achieve the coveted result of getting Clark in trouble. It sounded a lot like the truth.

Back to Clark . . . who now admitted, "Yes, I took the bike. But I lost it."

Lost it? LOST IT?

He swore he had no idea how he lost it or where he was when he noticed he lost it. ARGH.

So, were we to punish him for lying? Or "reward" him by withholding punishment because our unmedicated ADHD child chose truthfulness on the second go-round? We aren't fast learners, so we decided just to have him work off the value of the bike in more outside labor over the summer. This equated to thirty-five hours of outside labor in the Houston heat. Added to his penalty for the falsified note, he now had FOUR hours of outside labor a day. He agreed to this as fair and got started for the day.

His three parents (mom, stepdad, dad) wrung their hands and worried, but ultimately decided that this sedentary computer-gaming boy needed the exercise, and both father and stepfather reported that they spent their summer days at Clark's age performing manual labor outside for their fathers. So, no cruel and unusual punishment. As far as cruel and unusual was concerned, I was actually more worried about the impact on the adults who would have to oversee the forced labor. This was going to ruin my summer.

But we are not yet through with this tale of woe. Oh no, not yet.

We still aimed to find this bicycle and bring it back to its mother ship—our athletic family's game room houses seven bicycles on wall hooks, looking sorta like the pods in *Alien*. Clark's dad offered continued help on his end.

Thennnnnnnn, days later, Clark called from his father's house. "Wellllllllll Mom, I looked harder in Dad's garage and found it."

OK, how big, you may ask, is this garage? Is it like the multi-acre museum/lab in Dan Brown's *The Lost Symbol*, or is it just a standard garage? Is it cluttered like Eric's great-aunt's house was after forty years of collecting *Time* magazines and Star Trek action figurines, or more like most people's messy but functional garages? The answer: standard two-car garage, super-neat.

"OOOOKKKKK," I said to prompt him to speak further.

Before I could even finish getting the word out, I heard Edward in the background. "Clark, own it."

Uh oh.

And Clark said, "Uh, I left it at school and Dad found it chained to the bike rack up there."

School had been out for two weeks at this point!! The dreaded untruthfulness had raised its head again, while zero tolerance was in force. Why would any child agree to thirty-five hours of outside labor in the summer in Houston rather than just going to look for the darn bike? His dad ultimately was the one who found it! This was quintessential Clark, and quintessential ADHD.

For the last lie, we canceled Clark's computer camp that week. That caused a 6.7-magnitude Clarkquake. A much more immediate consequence, a much bigger impact. See Pamela learn, see Pamela try again.

For the sake of peace, we sent him to see my parents for a few weeks to cool off. He visited them on their farm for two weeks and the penalty remained in force there. During week one, he assisted my father. Clark learned to drive the big tractor, which he used to cut fields of grass and mow the four-wheeler path. The next week, he helped his grandmother pack up the home of his great-grandmother. His paternal grandfather came to visit him in Houston when Clark returned, and Clark assisted him for an additional two weeks. The work and the bonding made for great experiences for everyone, grandparents and grandchild alike. That got us through half the summer. The rest is a blur, but the yard sure looked nice.

Do our kids lie to us? Well, I once was a kid, and folks, I lied. I assume our kids get away with lying to us, too. We do the best we can, though, and they're awfully good kids, even that darn Clark.

## SOMETIMES I CRY.

For all that Clark finds a challenge, there are a few things he does better than anyone I know.

He returns to center.

He forgives me.

I wish I didn't have to know how good he is at these two things. It's already painful enough to watch him hurt at other people's hands, much less my own. To see him go through friendless years with no birthday parties or sleepovers, no pick-up ball games in the park, no casual drop-ins to play Xbox.

Or to see him hurt himself. It is excruciating to hear him say, "Mom, it's just so hard to be me. If you could just feel what it is like inside me, you'd see. It's really confusing, it's really fast." Of course, he'd say this at the same time he protested that he didn't want to take his meds because they made him feel like someone else. But, still, I ache for him, and I think I almost understand.

So, yes, I am angry at the people who overlook his awesomeness, who see only the negative. But I am mostly angry at myself.

Angry for all the times I lost patience with his lack of focus and easy distractibility and yelled at him. Yelled until he cried. Yelled until I knew that I, the one he trusted most and needed to rely upon, had wounded him.

I remember when he would lose control, when he would scream and hit the wall with a Transformer toy, and I would lose my temper. "Take that to your room, Clark! You will not act that way around the rest of us," I'd order, even as I knew that I needed to be the calm in the eye of his storm and help him find his way back to a safe place.

I remember all the times I hit the end of my endurance with his impulsivity and insensitivity, when I let him see me cry, when I spoke the words of my frustrated brain and battered heart aloud in his presence. I see him diminishing in size in my mind's eye. I see him folding inward. I know I did that to him.

I remember throwing things across the room when I couldn't get him to stop lying, the book thudding on the couch, the coffee cup shattering on the floor as I raged. I can see his crumpled face, scared eyes, and the back of his bowed head as he walked away to hide his tears. But I couldn't stop the angry words in my head.

*Why? Why does he lie to me? What is wrong with me as a parent that I can't instill an ethical sensibility in this child? Is he patterning himself after something missing in me? Is he a morally deficient person? I know what the doctors say, I know what the literature says, but all of this is outside my understanding.*

Clark seemed intuitively to know when I was at my worst, and it was then that he'd sink gleefully down with me. Sometimes I'd insert my husband as a buffer between Clark and me.

"Get him completely away from me," I would beg Eric.

"Why do you do this to your mother when you know she's having a rough time?" Eric would ask Clark.

"Huh?" Clark would answer.

My former mother-in-law, Clark's paternal grandmother, once told me that she could recall not a single night in her years as a mother that she did not kneel by the bathtub in tears, asking for God's forgiveness and a chance to do better the next day. I could relate, but in my heart, I knew I had failed Clark as a mother.

Failed **Clark**. Not my other kids. I get mad at my daughter and stepchildren at times. I raise my voice. I inform them of the dire consequences of their actions. Those times are rare, though. And never, not once, has my self-control shattered into millions of razor-edged shards like it has with my beautiful, sensitive son.

I have failed Clark as a mother at times.

And I wept then, as I weep now over my laptop. How on earth could I have hurt him so cruelly? I'm a good person. Ask anyone.

Whenever these moments occurred with Clark, it would not take many hours, and sometimes only minutes, before I found myself humbled and prostrate.

*I can do this, God. You saw fit to give a Type-A, slightly-OCD, quick-tempered woman this boy. I can do better. I will do better. Please help me.*

No matter what else I do wrong, I think I get one thing right: I always, always, always confess my short-comings to my son. I explain. I try to teach. I waste way too many words on a kid who I lost after "I'm so sorry, Clark. I was wrong. I love you."

His response? 100% of the time?

"That's OK, Mom. It's no big deal. I love you, too."

And once, branded on my memory, as I stood before him with tears running down my cheeks when he was fourteen?

"Please don't cry, Mom. It's my fault, not yours. I know how hard I make it for you. I make it hard for me, too."

*Oh, God, the question is not Why did you saddle two such different creatures with each other, it's How could you have blessed me so, have given me this resilient, kind soul and used him to mold me into a better person?*

Now, I am not a churchy kind of person. But there are times I know God sees my heart and speaks straight to it. And I promise you, the words he puts upon it, I hear as clearly as if he were sitting in front of me on my green garage-sale love seat speaking to me aloud.

"Forgive yourself as Clark and I forgive you. Love yourself as Clark and I love you. Marvel at and love this passionate, centered child. I believe in you."

Sometimes I cry. But only in between the times I marvel at my son and laugh. My son is a wonder, a love of a boy who wants a hug every day before and after school, his head tucked over and on top of mine. I am not worthy, but I will continue to do my best, and know that it is usually good enough.

For all of us.

# I'M PRETTY SURE THIS IS INAPPROPRIATE.

Clark and I saw these by the cash register at our local Blockbuster. I asked the cashier what he thought about Hot Mama and he said, "I think I'd stick a peppermint in and eat it like a lollipop."

I am not kidding. You can ask my (damaged) son.

I am pretty sure this is inappropriate, and I'm a certified expert in what is inappropriate, at least according to the state court in Bexar County, Texas. It's a long story; just trust me on it.

Way to go, Blockbuster!

To those of you worried that these risqué snacks might pickle Clark's brain, I must admit that I might have done that already myself. When Clark and Susanne were only eleven and nine, I took them to see *Talladega Nights* in the theater. It cracked me up, but I spent most of the movie blushing with my hands over my own eyes and ears. I wish there had been someone to do the same for my kids, but the only other person there was my mother, whose hands were over her own eyes.

I'd feel guilty about this, except . . . come to think of it . . . you can rent *Talladega Nights* at **Blockbuster**. Maybe I can blame it on Blockbuster.

Recently, I rented *Youth in Revolt* and allowed my teenagers to watch it unsupervised. When I watched it later, I was horrified to discover that most of the movie glorified teenage sex and criminal behavior. I know— Mother of the Year! It occurred to me that I'd probably need therapy to deal with the thought of my kids watching it—but really, I wanted to complain to Blockbuster.

Then I cleaned Clark's room.

I do not make it a habit to clean Clark's room, or even to go into it, if I can help it. In fact, I don't go upstairs to the "dormitory" where our three youngest kids live any more than absolutely necessary. My slightly-OCD brain short-circuits when I can't see the bedroom floor, and when I stripped the sheets off Clark's bed and discovered a *Sports Illustrated Swimsuit Edition* stashed between his mattress and box springs. I studied the cover carefully to figure out where my child could have gotten such contraband.

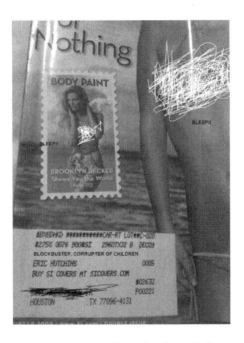

You can imagine my dread when I discovered the common link. I don't know who this Eric Hutchins is, but I am calling Blockbuster to complain about him IMMEDIATELY.

## IT'S ALL IN THE FAMILY.

Our family has ADHD.

Technically, only Clark has ADHD, but he shares. Sometimes in a good way, and sometimes in a bad way. Sometimes his pain hurts the rest of us a lot more than it hurts him.

Isn't that what the parent is supposed to say *to* the child, not *about* him? Whoops.

Want examples? When Clark was in third grade, I devised a wonderful poster board game for his life. If he completed life successfully that day — no dishonesty and no missed assignments — he would move one space forward. If not, he moved back one. I put tons of "Move two spaces forwards" on it, and prizes of all types every few spaces. Some were praise prizes, some were experience prizes, and others were loot.

Clark went backwards.

I was shattered. Even my most positive parenting had no impact. (Gee, you think he had ADHD??? This was pre-diagnosis.)

His younger sister was crushed that she didn't get a game board. We wrestled with it. At nearly six years old, she would slay the game board concept. We would go broke. We finally gave in, though. Luckily, she was young enough that I could sneak a simplified, prize-poorer version past her.

The smallest accomplishments at school earned Clark raves, but his sisters performed flawlessly with little intervention and fanfare—until we would catch ourselves and over-praise them in compensation.

Clark's daily bobbles absorbed our attention. We were constantly on edge, losing our patience, regrouping, and coaxing him along. At our worst moments, home was a tense place to live.

"Duck!" Clark got three zeros today.

"Run!" He stuck his Concerta under the microwave instead of swallowing it.

Once, Clark swore on MY life that he had packed his medication for our Christmas trip to the grandparents' house. Despite my repeated instructions to get it, he had to run back into the house minutes before we pulled out of the driveway at 5:00 a.m. Even so, the car pulled to a screeching halt half an hour later when we realized it was impossible for him to have it with him—it was in our bathroom. Still, we quizzed him on where he'd found it and ordered him to produce it. He couldn't, we turned around, and we got to the grandparents an hour late. It wasn't the end of the world. In hindsight, I should have made it easier for him to back out of his lie and turn for the truth.

The lows may be low, but the highs are higher. And don't the idiosyncrasies of *each* family member, not just those of the ADHD child, make an impact on the group? Our girls are positively bipolar as teenagers, with the requisite drain and drama. My husband has migraines that leave him a blubbering nerve end. Thank God, I'm devoid of imperfections, or we'd really be in trouble. All we can do is accept the negatives and celebrate the positives.

Clark's biggest impact on our family? He makes us laugh—with him, at his antics, at his wildly creative and zany sense of humor. "I like cheese and I'm a dog" he has announced so many times, apropos of nothing, that as soon as we hear "I like ch—" we scream "NO!" and laugh. He's just as likely to swing and miss, but when he connects, he's the funniest one in the house.

He has taught his sisters empathy for their peers, some of whom have ADHD or other challenges like dyslexia. Because of him, the girls know that those kids are probably at least as smart as they are.

Yep, we have ADHD at our house. Thanks for sharing, Clark.

# TO MED OR NOT TO MED

My father is a physician and Clark had a good pediatrician, so for most of his early years, like an ostrich, I stuck my head in the sand and assumed someone would tell us if we needed to worry about anything.

But I saw signs of trouble every day, from the time Clark was very small. He waggled his left hand incessantly, ran in circles, and would sometimes draw a long, gasping breath with his eyes wide with excitement rather than speak. He did not engage with other kids as I expected him to, as my daughter did. He wanted to be *around* them, but he didn't want to play with them. He had terrors. Terrors that you might expect, but bigger. Terrors of roller coasters. Terrors of scary scenes in TV shows. Terrors of loud noises. When the terrors got to him, he would run around fluttering his left hand and covering his ears and eyes with the other.

Diagnosis became an issue early in elementary school, but Clark's dad resisted having him tested. He feared Clark would be labeled, and he didn't trust medication or its side effects. He told the story of how he'd had to use his own life skills to succeed in college without a pill for a crutch, and how hard it was for him; he wanted Clark to do (to be able to do) the same. My own secret fear was not that Clark had ADHD, but that he was autistic.

But out of naiveté, I concurred. I assumed that we could help Clark enough through structured parenting that he could succeed. We privately sought out a diagnosis from a non-specialist on the small island where we lived, and the counselor gave us a conservative opinion: Clark's IQ was genius-level, but he was disorganized.

We learned how to help Clark with organizational skills. We obtained materials on the ADHD that we *insisted* to others Clark did not have, and studied up on how to parent him better. It didn't work well then, and it worked less with every passing year.

Whether Clark's more problematic behaviors were the result of ADHD or simply matters of personal choice became a point of contention, even of competition, for me and Edward. We took opposite ends of the rope and pulled until we were raw. Edward insisted that Clark could not control behaviors that I saw as choice-driven; I was adamant that Clark was choosing to behave badly.

I know now that Edward was usually right, and I was so, so wrong. He saw Clark's "refusal" to write down his homework assignments as evidence of an overwhelmed mind that crawled into its hidey-hole when faced with a task too complex for it to handle, but I couldn't understand why Clark would defy a direct instruction to write words on a piece of paper. It makes me sad to think of the perspective a diagnosis would have given me, but that spilt milk spoiled a long time ago.

There were things we agreed on. We both saw that Clark's addiction to computer games, and angry withdrawal when he had to quit, were brain-related. And Edward was right about something else: My frustration and anger over Clark's ADHD-related behaviors made everything worse.

For Clark. They made everything worse for Clark.

Post-divorce, and after we had moved to Houston, we sought counseling for both kids, but focused on Clark. His counseling sessions quickly turned into life skills and organization assistance, and provided an outlet for his non-divorce-related feelings about middle school, a horrible time for any ADHD kid. Through this counselor, we found the doctor who prescribed the meds that changed Clark's life.

Diagnosis was a stretch for Clark's father and me to seek, so it isn't a surprise that treatment challenged us as well. I would have started Clark on meds much earlier, but I deferred to Edward's strong feelings on the subject, and I don't regret it. Clark needed our full support, to have his parents united on decisions about his care and treatment. I was there to buffer Clark and to help him. Had his situation worsened, I would have insisted on the medications, but we didn't make the meds choice until he was nearly fourteen.

Clark resisted the Concerta from day one. He said it made him feel less creative, more controlled and re-strained. We spent his first year retrieving the pills he'd stashed in his backpack, in his drawers, under the microwave, in baskets, and in the closet. We still occa-sionally find them.

It was an expensive rebellion, but after nine months, he came to appreciate how they helped his performance, and by sophomore year, he would text me from school to bring his pill if he missed it. Success! It was short-lived, though; by his junior year, he was back to resistance. But still, more days than not, he semi-voluntarily took the pills.

He was still symptomatic on the Concerta, but the change in his focus and impulsivity was dramatic. For the first time ever, when he was asked to do something, he could walk away and do it. He still could not handle a list, but baby steps were good enough for us!

The only real side effect Clark experienced was disrupted sleep, which we were able to offset with occasional doses of melatonin. Melatonin has traditionally been used to replace depleted stores in aging adults to help them sleep, but it is effective on young kids with neuroatypicality, too. It's safe and it works for us—especially when we make sure Clark takes his Concerta as early in the morning as possible. If it gets past 9:00 a.m., we just skip a day.

Clark forgets his meds with some regularity, but just as often, he stumbles into the kitchen for a glass of water and his "performance enhancing drug," or PED as he calls it, as soon as he wakes up, without prompting.

I have regrets, for sure, about how we handled our early struggles and Clark's diagnosis and treatment. But most of all, I wish we had been able to make the decision to seek a stimulant prescription treatment sooner. Well, that, and that I'd known there were generic alternatives that would work just as well as the name brand.

I know that many kids feel ADHD and its related or co-morbid disorders are a stigma, and that to admit you take meds for them is akin to announcing you are a giant freaky loser, but not Clark. He is fairly open about both the ADHD and the medicine. Still, he yearns for a life without it. Someday, I tell him. Someday.

# "THERE'S NOTHING TO EAT AROUND HERE."

So who knew that the red dye in Pop-Tarts was con-tra-indicated for ADHD kids? Not me, apparently, since Clark gnoshed on them for breakfast every day one summer. Our psychiatrist enlightened me on the perils of red dye and a bunch of other confusing food issues at a med check visit one afternoon. I scribbled notes on an ATM slip: Proteins in the morning. Carbs at night. A little coffee is a good thing. Organic is ideal. NO RED DYES! Etcetera, etcetera, etcetera.

We still had three teenagers and four pets in the household, and I operated under the slop-line theory at mealtime. Eat what I fix, all'a'ya, or fix your own. Which they frequently did, opting for chicken strips and french fries, or half-baked chocolate-chip waffles. Gross and grosser. It was time for a change. A big, big change that I suspected only my husband and I would like.

But change was bad, and healthy change was worse. Like the day-of-the-week vitamin organizers I bought for everyone at Target, which none of the kids used without two live witnesses and a cattle prod. *Epic fail, Mom.* Our meals had sunk to the lowest common denominator of teenager-approved food, and when only the grownups ate the good stuff, we quit making it. But that didn't solve any problems, for the kids or for us.

Eric and I consider ourselves mediocre endurance athletes, but every mile our middle-aged bodies log on the road of life hurts worse if we aren't eating well. Eric has high cholesterol and blood pressure. Migraines plague us both. Gluten and sugar make my stomach and body hurt. (I am a devotee of Dr. Hotze and bioidentical hormones, but that's a topic for another day).

Mindful of the vitamin debacle, I picked up a copy of *Cooking Light: The Essential Dinner Tonight Cookbook.* The cookbook contained 350 healthy meals with instructions easy enough even for Clark to follow. They listed exactly what to do on each dish and in what order. "While the pasta boils, prepare the sauce. As the sauce simmers, grate the cheese . . ." It was foolproof.

So we announced that each family member would pick a menu at the beginning of the week. With five of us, that meant two free nights left over for junk—junk nights are key to our success. Everyone vowed to honor the selections of other family members.

Here's the shocking thing: The plan worked. The kids loved it. Excuse me—the *young adults* loved it.

Noticeably absent was any kvetching about food. The excitement level about picking and trying something new reached unforeseen highs, even for the child that had eaten only chicken, french fries, and waffles for the past nine months.

You know that daily text from Clark, "What's for dinner?" Now when we get it, it's followed by, "Whose night is it to pick? Is it my night? The stuff I picked rocks!"

I know, this too shall pass, but I'm still reveling in my one tiny success.

And no one's missed the Pop-Tarts yet.

# ME, ACCOMMODATING?

*Disability accommodations* is, to me, a term with multiple connotations. As an employment attorney and human resources professional, I strategize routinely with people about reasonable accommodation of disabilities at work. Large-screen monitors for the visually impaired. Desks under which wheelchairs fit. Modified seating for back conditions. And the like.

As a member of the special needs parenting community, accommodations mean public school Individual Education Plans and 504 Plans. It means evaluations, qualification, meetings, and appeals. You can get loads of this kind of advice from the informative articles listed in my Resources chapter.

What you won't get is much experience-based advice from me on IEPs or 504s. Why? Because as Clark's mom, accommodation means head-butting with my son, as he begs, "Don't do this to me, please," and tears. Mine, usually.

Clark hates accommodations.

In theory.

In practice, he probably doesn't realize how often he has benefitted from them when they were freely given by caring teachers without his notice.

Like the time when we lived on St. Croix in the U.S. Virgin Islands and he took a stick and whacked down all the rare native barrel cactus along the trail to the summit of Buck Island National Park. He acted on impulse, enjoying his moment full-out. Every ten yards or so was a stand of barrel cactus, so green and prickly and inviting. The stick in his hand felt so powerful. He was king of the island, striking down his enemies!

Except that the cactus were protected, and the park was patrolled.

Parental efforts to catch him, stop him, and hustle him away before the park ranger arrived were completely outside of his consciousness. We realized that confession wouldn't bring the cacti back, decided to tamp down our guilt, and took off for home.

In Clark's eyes, no one helped him. He stood alone, victorious.

As if.

And so it is with most of his teachers.

When Clark was in first, second, third, and even fourth grade, his teachers voluntarily accommodated him without us even asking. These kind, experienced professionals knew how to work with all the wonderful differences of the kids in their classrooms, and they tried to bring out the best in each of them. We hit a bobble in fifth grade, but I can say with assurance that since then, anytime we have made Clark's teachers aware of his special needs, they have cooperated to the best of their abilities. Color us among the lucky ones if you must, but I think we are the rule rather than the exception.

The kinds of accommodations his teachers have given willingly over the years have been simple. They understood where he should sit: not in high traffic areas. Not near the beautiful distractions of the window. Up front, near them. His teachers usually figured out how to keep him present. A tap on his book, a walk by his desk, even a light touch on his shoulder. They made eye contact with him. They emphasized key words, used inflection, stressed when things were important. In his younger years, they coached him. *Underline the important words. Write down your assignments in your binder every day. Clean out that backpack.* They assigned him errands, they let him hand out papers. They explained themselves clearly and broke instructions into chunks for him, then followed up to be sure he understood. They stayed in contact with us.

We gave Clark accommodations at home, too. We helped him clean out his backpack each week and helped him check it each day (at least up through his freshman year in high school). We assisted him and provided stimulus for him to organize his own room. We coached. We coaxed. We counseled. We made checklists. I printed fill-in-the-blank homework and assignment sheets each day during middle school for him to complete and bring home for discussion. We monitored his study environment and required his siblings to honor his space without distracting him. We kept him off the addictive computer games, even though he made us pay dearly for it. We gave him extra completion time and tolerated lower scholastic performance from him than from his siblings. Clark probably thought these lovingly-given accommodations felt like punishments at times, but they were anything but.

Isn't this the way it goes for many of us, though? We're all the product of efforts made on our behalf, whether we realized it at the time or not. Our parents made efforts, our teachers made efforts, friends and co-workers helped us. The greatest fallacy in the world is "I did it all on my own." What an insult to those who supported you without you ever having to ask! I look at the privilege of my own upbringing—involved parents, great schooling in Amarillo and at Texas A&M and the

University of Texas, socioeconomic advantages that impacted my health and wellness such that I was able to take advantage of my privileges, and great connections. I was accommodated, in the sense that people tried to help me.

Take the example of Clark's tenth-grade English teacher, who saw the real Clark and didn't want to let him go from her class, even when he was doing poorly in the pre-Advanced Placement English program (yes, due to missed homework). Keep in mind that his high school has over three thousand students. This woman took the time to inform me, to know my child, and to gently encourage the parent as well as the student—it shows a woman doing her job, plus a little bit, which is almost more than we could ask for, especially in a gigantic public school and with a student like Clark, who teachers since kindergarten have found to be a real challenge. For your reading ease, I've put the email in chronological order reading down:

***

-----Original Message-----
From: Ms. B
To: Pamela Hutchins
Subject: Clark's English grade

I just want to make certain that you have been checking GradeSpeed for Clark's current average. He has really slipped, as his current average is 61. I just spoke to him about this. He said it was the homework sentences. I'm concerned about his average. He said he will need to take the final exam early, which is fine with me. I asked him to come one day when he can devote time to study before this final; he should make it a day when he does not have other difficult finals to take. Just let me know the day. He needs to do well. He is a very smart young man and should be doing much better. Let me know if you have questions.

Ms. B

-----Original Message-----
From:Pamela F. Hutchins
To: Ms. B
Cc:Edward Jackson, Eric Hutchins
Subject:Re: Clark's English grade

Thank you Ms. B. We are painfully aware. We have battled exactly this type of performance since kindergarten -- big brain doesn't translate to classroom but does get a little better every year, and certainly his ADHD struggle makes it no easier. We have reinforced the need to do extremely well from here on out and to seek out help, and he has chosen a day for his test where his other class is PE. He really wanted to take the pre-ap classes and finds them so much more interesting than his normal classes, but we are

really leaning toward regular classes at the semester as we are always on the brink of disaster. He does enjoy your class, and we really appreciate your communication and concern.
Pamela Hutchins

-----Original Message-----
Ms. B wrote:

I would hesitate to put him in the academic level. Of course, that is your decision, but from my experience in teaching that level, the atmosphere is not always conducive toward higher level thinking. I have several students for whom I would encourage such a change, but Clark is not one of them. Of course, Clark has to be willing to put forth effort, and if he is not, he will not be successful at this level. Thank you for your kind words and your support.
Ms. B

-----Original Message-----
**From:**Pamela Hutchins
**To:** Ms. B
**Cc:**Edward Jackson; Eric Hutchins
**Subject:**Re: Clark's English grade

Thank you. We have never found anything positive or negative that truly motivates Clark, so whether he will choose to put in the work is the big question. He has said he will come to tutorials for the next two weeks. I hope he shows up. Could you please confirm whether he attends? The closest things we have found to motivational for him are a)interest b)Texas A&M admission. If you notice anything that appears to be working, let us know! :-) Have a good last few weeks before break--it's crazy times, I'm sure!

-----Original Message-----
From: Ms. B
To: 'Pamela Hutchins'
Subject: RE: Clark's English grade

I'm sure grammar does not inspire his interest, and as a faithful Longhorn, A&M anything is out of the question. He appears to have enjoyed *The Count of Monte Cristo;* I'm afraid *Jane Eyre* may not be as entertaining. I'll see what I can do if you decide to leave him in here. I will let you know if he comes next week. Enjoy your holidays as well.
Ms. B

***

Yay Ms. B!

So, my son chafes at the word accommodations. He refuses to consider asking for help, in high school, in college, or with the SAT/ACT.

But accommodations is not a dirty word. Accommodations are already there.

And, Clark's attitude or no, if he needed more, in the way of IEP or 504, I would not hesitate to march in to his school and ask for it.

Neither should you, or your child.

# L E A N  O n  M e

Remember how I mentioned I'm not a joiner, back when I admitted that Clark prompted me to take care of my alcohol issues? Well, I'm not. I am really, really not a groups kind of person. So the first thing a kindly phone rep with our insurance company suggested to me when I learned Clark might have ADHD?

A group. A support group.

I. DON'T. DO. GROUPS.

My idea of a support group is calling my mommy. If she isn't available, I get out the Blue Bell ice cream. Besides, at the time I still lived on an island in the middle of the Caribbean. There were no ADHD support groups less than a Guiness Book of World Records swim away.

We moved to Houston and Clark's new counselor recommended, yep, a support group.

"Bad idea!" I screamed at him. In my head.

I took the paper he held out to me. I glanced at the long list of groups, some local chapters of CHADD (Children and Adults with Attention Deficit Hyperactivity Disorder) and ADDA (Attention Deficit Disorders Association). Both of them are great groups, but I'm not a joiner, so I folded the paper in half and placed it carefully in my purse. As I exited the building, I looked all around me to make sure no one was watching, then dropped the paper in the trash and headed for the parking lot.

I really don't do groups.

Things with Clark got harder. I started writing about it. I do "alone with a laptop" pretty well, which sometimes makes up for not doing groups, especially when my mom isn't around or I run out of Dutch Chocolate. I wrote and I wrote and I wrote, and then I started clicking this button in my blogging software called "publish."

And something magical occurred.

Without ever realizing what was happening to me, I got sucked into a community. A community of parents with computers and internet connections who talked to each other through their blogs, Facebook, and Twitter. My community revolved around the blog of my friend Penny Williams, a co-author with me in *Easy to Love but Hard to Raise*, and the founder of {a mom's view of ADHD}. Penny invited me to join her community of writing mommas.

It's not a group. It's a community. A community is way different.

We don't have meetings. Unless we want to. But we call it going out for coffee or having a tweet-up; it's much more fun than a meeting.

We support each other. We advocate for each other. We cheer each other on, empathize, and answer questions for each other. We provide access to expert information, reading material, helpful videos, and useful products. It's really wonderful.

Once when Penny was having a terrible day, an ADHD momma low, we started a day-long campaign to celebrate the awesome traits of our ADHD kids. For twenty-four hours, members of our community posted pictures of their beautiful children's beaming faces, of their kids posed with kittens and jumping into swimming pools. Proud parents got the chance to brag about the traits that harried teachers and the condescending mothers of perfect little overachievers never saw. We told each other about our WonderKids and rejoiced together about what made them unique, special, and loved. I adored being a part of it.

Yeah, I know. It sounds a lot like a support group.

I don't want to talk about it.

# PICKY, PICKY, PICKY

After doing every one of these things wrong with my own ADHD teenager, I share with you here my top eight tips for picking classes for your ADHD highschooler:

1. <u>Later = better</u>. If your child takes ADHD medications, chances are that first period won't be his or her best performance period. Try to steer away from the substantive. P.E. would make a great first period class!

2. <u>Less homework = better</u>. Most of us find homework to be the Achilles' heel of our ADHD kids, so talk to the counselors, other parents, and older kids to identify classes that count homework as the smallest percentage of the final grade.

3. <u>Extra credit = better</u>. Your child is going to fail to turn in some assignments. Find teachers that offer extra credit or opportunities to turn in late work for partial credit.

4. <u>Experience = better</u>. Identify the teachers with experience working with neuro-atypical kids. Avoid teachers described as rigid or those that are unknowns.

5. <u>Interesting = better</u>. Search for classes and teachers that reward creativity and assign interesting projects. Shy away from teachers that grade on whether kids bring the right materials to class.

6. <u>Computer-driven = better</u>. For most of the ADHD world, handwriting is an issue. I find that my WonderKid works best verbally, next best by "keys," and least well with his left-handed penmanship.

7. <u>Easy 100's = good</u>. After all the times Clark's GPA has been challenged with atrocious grades, usually due to homework, I like an occasional easy A. Clark dropped Human Services (a.k.a. sewing), which he hated, for P.E. so he could shoot baskets with his

friends. How far I have come that my reaction was "Yay! Easy 100!"? Unless he forgets his gym shorts.

8. <u>Study hall = good</u>. Last but not least, consider a study hall period. Homework done in a supervised environment without the distractions of home and the push-pull of the parent-child relationship is a wonderful thing.

You're looking for teachers that can appreciate that your child is an outside-the-box thinker, teachers whose repertoire already accommodates all kinds of minds. And it sure helps if your easily distracted child likes the subject matter.

I wish I'd been smart enough to think of these things before I helped Clark pick his first two and a half years of classes in an enormous high school. Call me a late bloomer—just don't call me to say Clark didn't turn in his homework.

# GAMING THE SYSTEM

Like many parents of ADHD teenagers, we have struggled with the pros and cons of gaming for years. For Clark, gaming is a drug, a very addictive, destructive drug.

His drug of preference? World of Warcraft, Call of Duty, and similar games. Casual, controlled, fifteen-minute-a-day gaming allows him to feel focused and achieve successes that aren't possible amid the frustrations of his everyday experiences. He can interact with people online much more easily than in the real world. It feels good.

Gaming is not the real world, however, and some studies show that gaming activates the brain's basal ganglia and makes the body release dopamine, a chemical that imparts a sense of well-being, resulting in a mental shift from Clark Kent to the WonderKid. ADHD meds work the same way. Gaming is a form of self-medicating for kids with ADHD, not unlike drinking and doing drugs are for some older kids and adults.

Gaming doesn't just impact people with ADHD, of course. We have a friend, a judge, who went on a forty-eight-hour gaming binge with his son and ended up in the ER with seizures. He was forbidden by the Department of Public Services and Motor Vehicles to drive for a year. And a couple in Korea let their live baby starve to death while they played video games for days on end — including, ironically, a game where they had to feed and care for virtual babies.

Without parental intervention, Clark will game to the exclusion of everything else. He won't stop for sleep or food. His real life suffers: schoolwork, relationships, physical activity, everything. If he can't game, he uses books in much the same way, and will read all night with a flashlight if we're not on top of it. Try to take the "drug" away, and he becomes aggressive, unhappy, angry, even physical. It is an addiction. I can relate.

In his first year of high school, even a little was too much for him. Gaming became all or nothing. He could not voluntarily pull himself away; he would play through a nuclear holocaust without looking away from the screen. It was dangerous to him, and bad enough that even he recognized that he had a problem. Our solution to the gaming dilemma was multi-pronged:

*Absolute abstinence from gaming.* Clark actually partners with us on this now, since he has matured enough to understand how much it hurts him. That doesn't mean he won't fall from grace, but he wants to be in control and have fewer bad things happen to him, so this has been an important development.

*Game-replacement therapy.* Clark joined the robotics team at school, where he can work with computers and electronics in a social setting and drive the robot. He derives a tremendous sense of accomplishment from this. This has been an astoundingly effective substitution.

*Get the body moving.* We signed Clark up for a personal trainer and he joined the football team. OMG, he joined the football team. Physical exhaustion helped! It centered him. And it made him too tired to stay up all night reading fantasy books or sneaking down to the computer after we were all asleep.

*Treat the chemical imbalance.* Clark takes Concerta, although "taking" it is a mandatory activity. He will forget it if he's not reminded, and he will skip it if he's not monitored. Our goal is to assist him with meds, but not to replace learning the life skills that he needs now and will need even more when he some-day goes off the meds.

Although Clark lost the positives of casual gaming, its absence from his life freed him from the negatives — and all that was left for any of us were the negatives at that stage. He gained real social contact through robotics and football, and the medication helped steady him. It focused him enough that he could have meaningful social interactions without some of the awkwardness that had characterized his middle school years, pre-medication. We were elated.

This was such an effective combination of solutions for our son's self-esteem that we threw a party for him and his robotics friends at our house soon afterwards, something we hadn't done since he was in fourth grade. That five-year gap represented some difficult years for all of us.

Freshman year, second semester — so far, so good.

# LAWNMOWER MAN

Clark navigates life with a faulty GPS.

I have said this before, but it bears repeating: ADHD blocks many of the signals you and I take for granted. One of the hallmarks of ADHD children is their inability to process a time frame other than the present. They operate on the four seconds left to live premise of "now" or "HUH." This present focus renders normal choice/consequences logic meaningless for the young ADHD child, and it improves only slightly as he matures.

Medication helps. Support helps. But Clark and other ADHD kids find it hard to process why lying to avoid unpleasant circumstances in the present will matter later. Later is *later*.

That doesn't mean they don't know the difference between the truth and a lie, that lying is bad, and that getting in trouble is unpleasant. They just automatically go with "Lie now and defer punishment."

So how do you tell an ADHD lie from a deliberate, manipulative falsehood with the maturing ADHD kid? It's pretty dang hard, let me tell you. Consider our lawnmower incident.

It was a Sunday, chores day at our house. Clark's assignment: mow the grass in the front and back yards. Clark had been mowing the grass for years. Well, we'd been *trying* to get Clark to mow the grass for years. He always had an excuse. The mower wouldn't start, it was out of gas, the bag was full, he needed a snack/drink/to go to the bathroom, there were mosquitoes, yadda yadda. He could wear a mommy down, even a tough attorney mommy like me, but we still made him go through the roughly three-and-a-half-hour process each week of the mowing season.

Lately, Clark had been making mowing less painful. Not painless, mind you, but less painful. He finished in closer to forty-five minutes the task that should take twenty minutes. A 75% reduction in time. We could live with that.

So, it was Saturday, and we asked Clark to mow. He went outside and fifteen minutes passed . . . no roar of the lawnmower. We heard the door slam and the familiar slap of Clark's flat-footed duck steps as he came to find us.

Deep breath. In through the nose, out through the mouth. I felt the tension gripping my chest wall, and I let it go. This time could be different.

"Uh, Mom?"

"Yes, Clark," I said, careful to keep breathing and not let the irritation show yet.

"Um, I can't get the mower to start."

"AGAIN?" I wanted to say, loudly, sarcastically. I didn't. "OK, son. But are you sure you put gas in it?"

"Uh huh."

"What?"

"Yes, ma'am."

"All right, let me try. But if I can start it, you won't get paid your allowance, and we'll add another chore."

This was a method we had used to great success over the past year. Since his little sister could start the mower, we knew he could, and we felt no guilt about adding a few consequences to his helplessness act. It might not have solved the problem, but it made me feel better.

"I know, Mom, but it really won't."

And lo and behold, it wouldn't. So we called for reinforcements. My husband couldn't start it, either. He checked the fuel. He flipped it over and wiggled and jiggled a few parts. He went into the shed and came out with some wire. He did unfathomable things to the lawnmower.

"Try it again, Clark. It should work now," Eric said.

"'Kay," Clark replied. He gave the mower a few manatee-like pulls. It was obvious his heart was not in it. Then, to his horror, the mower started. Eric gave him a military salute, and Clark shuffled off to mow the yard with the speed and demeanor of a pallbearer.

"What did you do?" I asked.

"It was missing a little spring; I just put a wire in its place. I'll have to run to Home Depot and get a replacement spring for a permanent fix," Eric explained. Thank goodness, God pairs women like me with mechanical men like Eric.

That evening I decided to gather up laundry for washing. Normally, I holler up the stairs for Clark, Susanne and Liz to bring their laundry down, but since none of them ever take the call to action seriously, they end up doing personal laundry mini-drills all week long. I was feeling magnanimous that day, though, so I trudged up the stairs and braved the chaos of the dormitory.

I waded over piles of clothes on the hallway, bathroom, and bedroom floors with mounting agitation. How did they ever find anything up there? How was I supposed to figure out was clean and what was dirty? Oh, so that's where my nail polish had run off to. And this array of dirty glasses accounted for the empty cabinets downstairs. Sigh.

We long ago decided to pick our battles and found through trial and error that rebellion quelled if the kids were allowed to trash their own space. They participated in a tidy downstairs and cleaned their own spaces biweekly, which meant Clark's room was a demolition site for thirteen and a half out of every fourteen days. It usually seemed a small price to pay, as long as I stayed on the first floor.

Well, I at least knew the clothes Clark mowed in were dirty. I picked his shorts up off his bathroom floor, and, as I did, something fell out of his pocket and made a tiny "plink" sound on the tile. I picked it up. A spring.

**A LAWNMOWER SPRING.**

My son had sabotaged the lawnmower to get out of mowing. As I stared at the spring in my hand, an unstoppable desire to laugh came over me. I'm a mother post-forty, and I laughed until I was afraid I needed to change my drawers, if you know what I mean.

Eric heard my insane cackling and ran up the stairs. He found me sitting on the bathroom floor, head leaned back against the door, tears coursing down my cheeks.

"You scared me! Are you laughing or crying?" he asked.

"Both," I said. I held the spring up for him to see.

Eric's laugh was appreciative. "He's getting smarter. Very clever. But not smart enough to throw it away, and now we're on to him. Sabotage. Oh my gosh." He sat down beside me and took my hand.

"This took too much planning. Not a spur-of-the-moment ADHD 'I can't help it' lie," I said.

"Absolutely. Pure teenage boy lie. The medicine is working. He's becoming more mature."

I giggled again. "How many parents laugh and consider it a good sign when their offspring sabotage machinery to avoid work?"

"There has to be a serious consequence. We're going to have to ground him," Eric said.

"I know. No more screens until summer. But let's put it off a few more minutes. I don't feel like being a big meanie yet. I'm enjoying this, in a sick and distorted way."

Five minutes later, we called Clark in. I held up the spring. At fourteen, Clark was 5'9" tall. He had beautiful, innocent, big brown eyes; he made wonderful eye contact and looked so sincere, usually. This time he looked at the spring like Bambi staring at the fire in the woods. *Danger! Run, Bambi, run —*

"I love you, but I'm going to have to kill you now," I said.

"Uh, Mom, uh—"

"Clark, if you were smart enough to sabotage the lawnmower, how in the world could you leave the spring in your pocket? Didn't you know I'd find it when I did laundry?"

In a rare moment of honesty, Clark said, "I never thought you'd go up to my room and get my clothes."

"Ah . . ."

Note to self: Must keep surprising the children, change up my game. This is how we keep them honest.

"So, I'm, uh, I'm sorry?"

"I hope so. You know the drill. Choice/consequence. Bring me your laptop. And choose better next time, son."

I pondered our household. One child grounded for skipping homeroom (twenty-three times), one grounded for lawnmower sabotage. We have a three out of five rule: At any given time, only three of our five kids can be happy and issue-less, max. As soon as one of them gets straightened out, another will dip into crisis, leaving us with the conundrum of how to root for one to rally at the expense of another one cratering. Thomas, Marie, and Liz were all doing great . . . all of *Eric's* kids . . . Susanne and Clark, my kids, were on the skids. Uh oh, I saw the common denominator here. I inhaled the scent of freshly mowed grass and looked at my husband.

"Honey, is it me?" I asked.

Eric smiled at me, his face earnest and supportive. "No more than it's me when both of yours are doing great and all three of mine implode. Remember, he'll have a wonderful assistant some day and everything will be just fine."

"I want to be a lawyer when I grow up," Clark broke in.

Eric looked at me and shook his head. "I take it back. It appears it's you after all."

Touché.

# CLARKAPALOOZA

What do you get when you combine Clark with 750 screaming teenagers, 65 robots and 10 pounds of face paint? The 2010 FIRST Robotics Competition, Lone Star Regional in Houston, Texas. FIRST (For Inspiration and Recognition of Science and Technology) and BEST (Boosting Engineering Science & Technology) hold annual multi-week-long robotics competitions.

If you don't already have ADHD before you go to a robotics competition, you'll experience it while you're there. Flashing lights, loud music, kids dancing the Macarena everywhere, and all the while an ongoing competition, complete with a big-screen scoreboard and an announcer on acid.

Clark joined the robotics club during his first year in high school. With his tendency toward impulsivity-induced injury—such as when he broke his arm by "accidentally" sticking it through the moving parts of an elliptical exercise machine, or the time he ended up with a face full of stitches after "accidentally" hitting himself in the face with a Louisville Slugger—we were concerned. Robotics involves blades, electricity, and moving parts. So far, so good, though.

And the caliber of kids he is around? Amazing. These kids are budding rocket scientists, seriously. Sponsors from the biggest companies in the world vie to get their names in front of this brain trust of future science, engineering, and technology superstars. Let me assure you that BP does not sponsor our daughters' swim meets! I think the message is clear: they want to hire these kids someday.

Even the lead-off speakers signal these students' potential. In March, the governor of Texas opened the program. In April, the head of NASA in Houston spoke to start the festivities. Both events play on cable channels.

The Lone Star Regional boasted sixty-five teams from as far away as Laredo on the border of Mexico and all the way to Louisiana. And oh, what teams they were: Iron Plaid, Gatorzillas, Kryptonite, Texas Torque, Robatos Locos, Discobots, the Finger Puppet Mafia, and Clark's own Scitobors, to name a few.

The screams of crazed kids filled the air. They weren't just competing for robotics awards—they were competing for pride. Some of the costumes rivaled

Hollywood movie wardrobes. Imagine the scene: sparkly disco capes, green spiked mohawks, gatorzillas, and my personal favorite, a kid in a giant robot costume with internal stilts. Even the sponsors were decked out in team wear. Our team was one of the smallest, and our kids restrained themselves a bit more than others, but Clark face-painted with the best of them.

For this competition, the teams built robots to do several tasks. 1) Score soccer goals, 2) Overcome bumps on the fields, and 3) Suspend themselves from towers. Each team has at least one adult to coach and assist, but the kids perform the bulk of the work. They build their robots under weight constraints and a set universe of parts to choose from. They must strategize which tasks they believe they can accomplish to score the most points and incur the fewest penalties. Most robots cannot make weight limit and do all three tasks well, so the teams specialize in one or two.

Clark's team did not make finals, which bummed them a little, but they improved with each round. They modified their robot to eliminate penalties and increase their goal-scoring opportunities. Team Captain Matt ran the group like a NASCAR pit crew. Clark drove the robot and — break away from those gender stereotypes here — his female team member ran the electronics through a laptop. Their team members cheered them on and helped with modifications.

Watching my ADHD son through this robotics season has made me appreciate the aspect of gaming involved in learning to drive and compete with a robot. This is real life, though, with a physical machine, live teammates to work with, and a cheering crowd of real-live humans. He has to get his hands dirty with actual tools between rounds, and if he doesn't remember to wear his safety glasses, he can hurt his eyes. He must interact effectively with team members to lobby for his strategy and ideas, and for them to convey the same to him about his driving.

He can put his hands on the computers he so dearly loves — there is a lot of programming involved — but he also has to translate his thinking into pure mechanics. The kids cut metal, they bolt, they tighten screws, they run wiring, they build a machine from the ground up and make it roll around a field at high speeds, running over obstacles and kicking soccer balls. He paints his face and gets excited about a team project.

Certainly, his medication helps him do robotics. On the days he sneaks off without it, he does not perform as well. He knows, though, that his team counts on him, and doesn't even try to skip meds on robotics days. The difference this activity has made in him is astounding.

I'll admit, I shook pompons as a cheerleader and ran track when I was his age. I didn't get it about robotics at first. I worried that my son, who already faced frustrations and challenges I did not fully understand, would doom himself to becoming the biggest dork at his high school. I could not have been more wrong.

Pre-medication and pre-robotics, Clark never even got in the game, whether it was lacrosse, school, or social interaction. Once he joined robotics, he was in the thick of it, with a bunch of super-smart, super-cool friends who treated him with respect.

Clarkapalooza.

Go Clark. Go Scitobors. Robotics rocks!

# THE OTHER STUFF IN CLARK'S ROOM BESIDES THE SWIMSUIT MAGAZINE UNDER THE MATTRESS

Clark is a mess.

You *think* your kid is mess, but I'm pretty sure Clark beats your kid up one side and down the other. I don't mean to brag or anything, it's just that this is one of the areas he puts his best effort into, and it really shows. We know an organized environment helps a distracted mind, but Lord help us, it's like he's allergic to tidiness. One minute his bedroom is neat and clean, and the next minute he goes in on a sock search and emerges from a maelstrom of clothes and books.

At the beginning of his sophomore year in high school, he had 12.5-hour football lock-ins for three-a-day practices[11], indoctrination, and brainwashing. Understandably, he was dragging ass a bit when he got home. The week before, he'd folded the family's laundry. It took him all day, but he assured me at the end of it that he'd done quality work. He batted his Bambi eyes at me and I, fool that I am, believed him.

A week later, my husband couldn't find any underwear. (A quick explanation about Eric and underwear, which I know he will appreciate: Eric changes underwear every time he goes near a bathroom. Wait, that's an exaggeration. OK: Eric changes his underwear every *other* time he goes near a bathroom. So he owns like seventy pairs. I'm not lying. But that week, he had ZERO pairs.) We panicked and I undertook a search and rescue mission on his skivvies.

I started in the laundry room and worked my way into the game room, where we keep the unfolded laundry on our ping-pong table (you really must get a ping-pong table—it can hold up to 20 loads of unfolded laundry), and on to the living room where Clark had done the folding. Nada.

---

[11] Meaning he stayed at the school for 12.5 hours, locked-in, for a full day of activities that included three practices, meals, naps, and various team meetings.

You know I don't go upstairs into the dormitory unless it's an emergency, but I thought about Eric squirming and miserable because he couldn't change his pants, and I sucked it up, because that's the kind of goddess wife I am. I climbed those stairs. I went into Clark's room. Normally, for the sake of a good laugh, I take pictures for my blog[12] of anything funny I encounter during my day.

But I could not bring myself to document the horror of his room, even for the sake of humor. I couldn't find the floor, and there was no way I would find Eric's seventy pairs of underwear without a gas mask and a jackhammer. Thirty cussing, spitting, screaming minutes later, I not only found a few pairs of my beloved's drawers, but I also found my clothes, my daughter's clothes, my stepdaughter's clothes . . . everyone's clothes but Clark's. There were clothes on his closet floor, on his couch, under his dirty clothes, and — wait for it — UNDER HIS BED INSIDE A LINEN BOX. All these clothes had been worn and washed within the last ten days. He hadn't just phoned this one in. Normally I would have gone all Psycho Mom at this point, but I knew it was too far gone for Clark to take care of it himself. I planned his "consequence" for his bad choice about the laundry, and

---

[12] *Road to Joy,* http://pamelahutchins.com/.

I congratulated myself on being the nicest mom in the history of the world, and I * CLEANED * HIS * ROOM!!! I know, I'm supposed to help him do this by himself, but with three-a-day football practices, I took pity on him. When I finished two hours later, I decided to do a little labeling to help the ADHD side of his brain keep the room in order for a coupla days.

When I was done, his room looked like it had been hit by a blue sticky blizzard. We had the big reveal after practice that day (right after our "Thou shalt perform slave labor for Eric this weekend without complaint" talk). I worried he would be mad about my clean-up and stickies, which in turn would have made *me* mad and would have shot the whole warm-fuzzy element to hell. He likes things to remain the same, even if they're cluttered and messy, and he takes time to deliberate and process his thoughts. I needn't have worried, though. He loved it.

He especially loved that I put his swimsuit edition back where I found it.

We never did find all seventy pairs of poor Eric's underwear. Maybe they were in the neighbors' yard with the missing poo?

# I'M WORN OUT JUST THINKING ABOUT IT.

Who knew?

All this time—fifteen years—and who knew?

It turns out that one of the most effective strategies to focus the ADHD brain, at least in our house, is to exhaust the body physically. Add exhaustion of the mind to that, and you're really rocking.

Our guinea pig, Clark Kent the WonderKid, wrapped up thirteen-hour days at school where his high school football team practiced three times a day. In the 107-degree-heat-indexed August days of Houston. Yikes.

Between their three 1.5-hour practices each day, the boys were in lock-down. They spent most of this time in brainwash mode: lectures, films, plays, conduct, rules and even teamwork/bonding activities (of course, they didn't call them that to teenage boys!). Clark stumbled home physically and mentally spent on day one.

But instead of behaving like a zoned-out zombie, he was simply . . . calm. Unruffled. Not buzzing and zipping around. *Capable. Helpful. Conversational. Thoughtful. Thinking about the next day.* HOLY CRAP. HE WAS PLANNING. HE PACKED A BAG. Not very well, but *baby steps, people!*

He kept up this regimen for six days, then the team slipped back to two-a-days in week two. Sure, he got sick from exhaustion, but that's what vitamin C is for, right? The important thing was he was so much less of all the things he normally is that we almost didn't know him. Woo hoo!

Kidding. Mostly.

Why didn't anyone ever tell me this was all it took? If you knew this and withheld it from me, I'm coming after you. Watch your back.

So on to the first day of school: he left the house at 6:45 a.m. and returned at 7:30 p.m. He only practiced football for two hours instead of five, but his mental workout was tougher. Result? He finished his home-work, he helped clean up after dinner, and he sang (to the annoyance of all of the rest of us) as he watched Monday Night Football.

The thing he was most of all?

**Happy**.

Color me optimistic about tenth grade.

# THIS HURTS ME MORE THAN IT HURTS YOU.

When I married Clark's father in 1992, I didn't know two things:

1. He had ADHD and
2. Our marriage would end after 12 years.

I'm not sure what impact knowledge of either fact would have exerted on my choices the year we married, but the fact is, marriage and parenthood involve lots of future unknowns. The past is certain.

We divorced because of our own issues, but like any couple that endures a difficult time with a child's disability, we lived under more pressure than we had expected when we said "I do." We will never know whether our marriage would have been easier if we'd made different decisions about Clark's diagnosis and treatment when he was very young.

Yet isn't it always something? Marriages will always face adversity, because people will always face problems. It's the human condition. Edward and I, like any couple, faced a variety of challenges. In the end, we simply decided we didn't want to go through life with each other.

Our divorce raised new issues. We would continue co-parenting our children together. How, though? Neither of us wanted to deprive the kids of time with the other parent, nor the other parent of time with the kids. But I worried about Edward's inconsistent parenting, especially when it came to Clark. And Edward worried about my frustration over and inability to understand Clark's ADHD. Two years into the divorce, we agreed to trust each other and stay flexible. This worked well for a few years. Until it didn't.

Hold that thought.

The divorce had an immediate positive impact on Clark. Nope, I'm not living in a dream world. The divorce broke his heart, and it had some expected negative impact, but it also helped him. Clark hated conflict and he couldn't tolerate raised voices. Picture him as a small child running away from our angry, fighting voices with his hands over his ears, slowing down to flutter his left hand and run in a circle, then resuming his flight. Divorce meant that the conflict was over. Full stop. Big sigh of collective relief.

Another benefit to him was that my frustration with ADHD was no longer exponential. I stopped feeling angry at Clark because he was acting like Edward. I know now that this played a role in my feelings before the divorce.

Since then, Clark's dad and I have done the best we can to split parenting time and duties equally. I think this makes us somewhat unique — so unique, in fact, that we confused our attorneys and the judge. But we wanted to send a clear signal to the kids that we love them equally and believe in the other parent's abilities.

How does this custody arrangement work in practice? For starters, it requires us to live within walking distance of each other. This is not a divorce book, so I won't bore you with the mundane issues, like "I preferred never to see this person again so why do I run into him at the Kroger grocery store and 24 Hour Fitness every week?"

Just joshing. Sort of.

Our custody arrangement works fine for our neurotypical daughter. She's organized and navigates the weekly transitions with ease, if not always with a perfect attitude. Some weeks she whines, "I don't want to go back and forth." But I'm lucky. Even when it isn't my week, she comes over after school and pesters me until her father comes to pick her up after work. The blessing and the curse of a home office!

The arrangement has never worked as well for Clark. He has enough trouble organizing himself in one space, and transitioning week by week is hard for him. We tried to set up environments in each home that required him to tote as little as possible back and forth, but the stuff that trips him up can't be duplicated. Does he have his worksheet from Algebra? Today is a robotics day — did he leave his shirt at the other house? It was clear that the strain of preparing to transition, transitioning, and failing in the transition stressed him out.

From day one, I petitioned his father for a primary space for Clark at my house, but Edward, understandably, didn't want to give up the time with him. Until recently, when he came to me with tears rolling down his face; the time had come to let Clark live at my house and spend every other weekend with Edward. It was a painful decision for Edward to make, but he did it in the best interest of his child.

And thank God. Clark needed it. As Edward explained to Clark and me, he has ADHD, too, and his was not the better household for Clark. He concluded that he could do best for Clark by giving him stability and stillness at La Hacienda de Hutchins.

Clark was elated. He adores his father, but he hated the stress.

So, how did the change go? Well, awesome, really. Clark is still Clark Kent, and he still has ADHD. But our collective stress level has plummeted. We have far fewer fire drills, running back and forth between houses, trying to determine where he left or lost what—usually his meds. He does his work in the same place at the same time with the same rules and same supervision every day. He suffers under the eagle eye of his very non-ADHD momma, which means an endless stream of prompts.

As in, "So Clark, what do you think you should do next? And then? And how about now? Did you write it down? Could you write it down? If I begged you on bended knee, would you consider writing it down? Would you just pretend to write it down so I could have a moment of peace? Thanks."

I'm very happy.

And so, it seems, is Clark.

# ROLLERCOASTERING

Up. Down. Up. Down. Down. Down. Up. Down. CompleteloopwhichwayisupdownupdowndowndownU P.

Life with that boy. As a high school sophomore, Clark transformed his manatee self into a 5'10" lean machine playing on his high school's 5A football team. 5A football in Texas means you're playing with the big boys. Three-a-day workouts exhausted and focused his scattered mind. Things looked good. Really good.

But what a difference a few days make.

Almost as soon as I tempted fate and the furies with my euphoria over his progress, Clark imploded. When school started and exercise waned, his behaviors reverted to startlingly bad, almost as if he were not on medication at all. He wandered in circles. He waggled his left hand. He blurted, he interrupted, and he aggressively drove everyone in the family insane.

Progress reports came in. We discovered failing grades in all five of his substantive classes. He announced he wanted to quit football.

Regroup time. Fast.

We suspected an inadequate dosage of his medication played a part. Clark objected to the meds increase, but he agreed the doctor would have the final say. We made a meds appointment. Could the five inches and forty pounds he'd gained in the last year have rendered his meds ineffective? The doc said no. She opined that dosage did not bear a relation to weight or density. However, she agreed he needed more and increased his dose.

She reiterated her caution against foods with dyes, especially Pop-Tarts and colored drinks. She advised protein in the morning, carbs and vitamins at night, and sleep. Lots and lots of sleep.

Good luck with that. As far as I could tell, Clark had not slept since he was a one-year-old. I'm serious. When Clark was nearly two and his little sister Susanne was born, well-meaning friends and loved ones told me to nap when Clark napped or I would get crazy tired. Clark, unfortunately, had napped his last nap by then. Ugh. To this day, he sleeps less than any of his family members. Thank God for the occasional melatonin, which we'd started years ago, but used as sparingly as we could.

Next, we attacked the schoolwork. Again, Clark raised objections.

"You said you'd let me do it by myself this year," he said.

"You will do it by yourself. But with accountability to us," I replied.

He began daily reporting (*again* — shades of yester-year). Slowly, the grades began to come up. The reasons for the Fs? Organizational issues, of course. A notebook left at a rival high school during a debate tournament. A book lost under a stack of mixed clean and dirty clothes that he had been told to put up. Etcetera, painful etcetera.

The straw that broke our humped backs, however, was football. Clark had insisted on playing football, despite almost zero football experience. He had just turned fifteen, but his physician expected him to reach 6'1" (which he did a year later, and then kept growing).

Size isn't an issue for him. Mental suitability is. It turned out that, despite already being ready for the NFL draft in his mind, Clark didn't like to hit at all. Or to be teased about being physically behind the other kids.

Meanwhile, he had fallen in love with debate. To his way of thinking, he should no longer waste all that time on football that he could spend on debate. We disagreed.

"You committed to the football team. You have to stick with it through the end of the semester. After that, your choice. Before then, you will not quit," I told him.

But forbidding Clark to quit did not stop him from engineering the situation for himself. On a game day, he found an excuse not to pick up his laundered uniform in time to board the bus. He told the other kids he was quitting and hid in the debate room.

Hmmm . . . earlier in the summer, he'd hid in the cafeteria rather than attend practice, but he had overcome his fears and rejoined the group. Would he this time?

We warned the coach of the situation. You would think the head coach of a Texas 5A football team with 170 players would have better things to do than deal with our uncommitted son, but the coach rocks, and he told us to have Clark come talk to him.

We sent Clark off to school the next day with a reminder: "Don't come home without talking to the coach. Don't just let this float to a foregone conclusion."

The day went by. Clark didn't go talk to the coach. No surprise, but still sad.

Somewhere over a long weekend of second-guessing himself, though, something amazing happened, something that had never happened with Clark before. He became introspective.

"Mom, I really messed up."

"Tell me more, Clark."

"I don't like playing football. I messed up, though. I shouldn't have done that. It's just that *I never succeed at anything.*"

Readers, I had never, ever heard Clark stay in a moment long enough to vocalize anything but a positive Superman-style self-perception. While it hurt my heart to hear him sad, I knew I could do something with this moment. Clark was here with me — a new Clark, a Clark with an ability to see the past and future, not just the now. I would like to take a moment to thank his doctor for the higher dose of Concerta. Hallelujah!

"Clark, remember yesterday when you came in second place in the novice cross-examination category in the debate tournament? You succeeded," I explained.

"I didn't win."

"No, you didn't. But you still improved and succeeded. Even though you succeeded, you didn't debate a perfect round. And if you had not entered the novice division, how do you think you would have done against kids who had a lot of experience?"

"Not as good."

"Right. That's what's happening in football. You are on teams with kids who have a lot more experience than you do. You don't have to be the best to be a success. You don't even have to be good. You just have to stick with it and improve, and you have succeeded. You already have succeeded."

"But I messed it up."

"Yes, you did. You didn't listen, you weren't honest in your actions, you violated our trust by acting against our instructions to go talk to the coach. You skipped a game with no excuse. Those things are not successes. But you can fix them. You can go back in to the coach and ask him for a second chance."

"He won't give it to me."

"Grown-ups are not monsters, Clark. He might or he might not, but he won't eat you. And to us, you will succeed just by going back in there and making it right. Even if you end up as the film guy or the water boy, you can succeed by not quitting."

"My grades suck. No one ever does stuff with me."

Ouch. That was mostly true.

"You'll pull them up. You always have before, and you're back on track. I know it's harder for you than your sisters, but you don't fail, Clark, you just walk a longer path to success. And I am sorry about the other boys. But things are getting better there, too. You have met tons of people through robotics, football, and debate. You have lots of new friends on Facebook. You went to Chick-Fila with a friend last week. You are getting there, son. Be honest, stick to it, and you will succeed in all of this."

On Monday, Clark did it. He went to the coach. He talked to him face to face. He explained why he did what he did. The coach sent him out to practice and told him to come back in twenty-four hours and tell him what he — Clark — would commit to do with pride and passion. He gave him a second chance, and he put the ball in Clark's hands. Whether he runs or punts, Clark succeeded in showing a step change in maturity.

I can't fix things for my son. I can't even tell when the challenges he faces relate to ADHD or belong to his own unique personality. I can only pray and hang on for the loops, ups, and downs. For this is our rollercoaster. This is Clark. This is life with teenage ADHD.

# NOT UP FOR DEBATE

And so it was that Clark discovered a new passion: debate team.

Up until now, arguing and gaming were Clark's top passions. These passions caused great household consternation—arguing with Clark can make you insane, and we were always arguing with him for one reason or another. We were all really tired of arguing with Clark.

The idea of Clark arguing on purpose with non-family members gave us hope. Might this be the outlet we needed to distract him or tire out his arguing mechanism? We prayed . . . but we also feared it would simply whip him into a perpetual arguing frenzy, with the added irritant of specialized debate terms and rules applied to our household discussions. So far, it looked more like the perpetual frenzy than the outlet. Lord help us.

Clark was the first debater in the family. He gravitated naturally to debate, probably thanks to his ADHD and argumentative nature à la paternal genetics. He assured me that, his father's contribution notwithstanding, he wants to be a lawyer like me. This was supposed to make me feel *better*. However, despite my misgivings about the perpetual frenzy of arguing, we attended his first debate tournament with anticipation.

Clark and his partner competed in the finals of the novice cross-examination category. The kids debated for over an hour and a half whether to withdraw U.S. troops from Okinawa. Their knowledge impressed me, and the intensity and helpfulness of the judges surprised me. Clark's team lost, mostly due to rookie errors in how to score winning votes. I can't pretend to understand it all. But none of that is really what interested me.

What hooked me? The stream-of-consciousness vocalization and demonstration of the ADHD mind by Clark Kent the WonderKid. While Eric marveled that Clark could apply any organization to his thoughts at all, I was blown away by his words.

In the middle of making a point and without taking a breath, Clark would blurt out, "I can't remember what I was going to say," and then go on to a new topic. Partway through it, he would interrupt himself with "But I don't know what comes next," and then bounce to another point. And just when he was on a verbal roll, he would cut it short and announce, "And I have no idea where I was going with this." One after another, he made excellent points and jumped willy nilly to his next thought, with these funny admissions and transitions.

Whew!

I sneaked a glance at the judges while he was impulsively admitting his confusion. They loved it, and they seemed to love him. Despite his rapid-fire delivery of a multitude of nearly-finished thoughts, his intelligence and flair for the dramatic stood out. Thanks, middle school theater teacher! Most of their post-match critique was a dissertation on how he could take his game up a notch. They didn't pay much attention to the other three debaters, including the two that won.

The other debaters came up to me afterward and said, "Your boy is going to be a rock star."

Will he? Can he overcome the ADHD enough? The main critique of the judges was that Clark made excellent points but never followed through on them. The debate was a microcosm of his daily struggle to come full circle and tie together all the information that flows through his mind. He lives in the moment, and all that wonderful info he blurted out in the debate was in the present. Tying it to something he had already said or should say later would be a monumental challenge.

Take chess, for example. Clark likes the idea of playing chess. He is astoundingly good at making a move for the best possible outcome on any given turn. But chess is a game of strategy over many, many moves, of thinking ahead to what your partner will do five, six, or seven steps ahead to set something up. Clark gives zero thought to the upcoming moves.

Still, things look good for debate. He's a natural speaker with great intelligence, and the bouncing-ball feel of debate matches the flow of his thoughts. I've never seen anything like it. That day, I felt like I knew him in a way I never had.

Can he apply rigor, organization, and planning to his delivery? Can he master his mind? He was debating with a very organized female partner, which helps. I suspect he can. I doubt many people will realize how hard it is for him, though.

After the match, we asked him why he'd made all the remarks about not knowing what to say next.

"Huh?" he asked.

"You know, all those times you told us you'd lost your train of thought?" I said.

"Um, I don't know what you're talking about, Mom."

Seriously. The kid has no recollection at all of saying any of them. I don't know what blew me away more—

hearing him say them or hearing him say he had no consciousness of saying them.

Wow.

"Well you did. And you were great!" I told him.

"If you say so. And thanks."

That boy. But you know what? He didn't argue with me about it.

# Rabbit, meet the white hat.

Clarkapotamus.

No, that's not a cuss word. That's one of the nicknames my husband has bestowed upon our youngest son. Others include Clark Kent, Clarkyopteryx, Clarkosaurus Rex, and Butthead. I won't tell you which one Eric calls him most often.

To me, he is just *that boy*.

Whatever name he goes by, Clark is always undeniably himself. Which means mayhem and chaos reign in his world (Google the lawnmower commercial for Allstate Insurance to get an idea of what I mean).

First semester of his sophomore year in high school was no exception. He managed to set himself up needing a 90 on his Algebra II final *just to pass the semester*, notwithstanding his A-B-range test grades and genius IQ.

Picture me shaking my head and wringing my hands with tears rolling down my face as I laugh hysterically.

Clark knew this final was do or die. Finally, finally, finally, he started availing himself of opportunities for at-school and at-home tutoring. He studied, he turned in completed work, and he spoke to the teacher without turning into a statue. Why must he wait to perform until the situation is dire? Argh.

I asked his doctor about this, and she didn't seem overly distressed. Nor did she offer a pill for it. Some help she is.

Clark studied more for that final than I have ever seen him study. And he argued less with Eric than he ever had before when Eric graded his practice tests and slashed his answers for sloppy errors or incompleteness.

And how did that kid perform on the final? In the class in which his six-week averages had been 61, 52, and 77 — with the 77 coming only after he realized he was up against the proverbial wall?

He made a 98. And was upset because he thought he should have made a 100.

*Sigh.*

I don't think he learned any lessons here about how sustained effort could make his life easier and better. He pulled a rabbit out of the hat once again. That *darn* boy.

Congratulations are in order, however. He avoided summer school and  three long, hot months of frustrated parents.

# I CANNOT TELL A LIE.

How do you explain a family like ours in what is supposed to be a hardly-truthful, totally-feel-good Christmas letter — a Southern tradition I dutifully follow? This is what our Christmas letter looked like the year Clark imploded, quit football, and got five Fs:

***

Some of us have called ourselves family longer than others. Some used to call us family and now don't. But whatever, whenever, and whoever, we are us. From all of us at our house, Merry Christmas to you.

We are celebrating our fourth Christmas as a Hutchins-Jackson household. Well, technically, it's the fifth year, but we added one more Hutchins about a year into the timeline, so we'll call the first year "Year Zero." Yeah, it's confusing. Deal with it.

So, the big question is, how did the year treat us? What silliness will I now regale you with, pretending only the good stuff counts? Well, all in all, I'd count it a success.

We started out and ended with five offspring. One of them is mad at us, but that's not unusual. Usually, in fact, several are at a time. One is heading back to graduate school, another graduated from college. One earned the first F in the family and skipped class 23 times, and her brother followed up with a feathered flock of FFFFFs on his fall report cards. One is about to graduate high school and another is about to graduate middle school. One quit football but discovered debate. Another scored a car and a boyfriend. It's been up down and all around. Fun. Crazy. Sad. Happy. Awesome.

Eric and I continue our fiery "there are no words for it" wonderful marriage. Seriously, pinch me. It's that good. (A moment to reflect on everyone that said we would never last. One word: wrong!)

His job is solid and he loves it. We both wish he traveled less. Someday.

My job is solid and I am grateful for it. We both wish I could write as an occupation instead of an avocation. Maybe someday. :-)

We still can't sell all the property we own in Lancaster, SC. Buyers, anyone?

Our athletic pursuits took a nosedive. Me: Plantar fasciitis. Him: work, travel, and health issues. We are determined to regain our triathlon mojo in the upcoming year.

I rewrote my first two novels several times. I wrote a third novel. I have agents circling (pray). I started a blog called *Road to Joy* about utter nonsense that thousands of strangers read for God knows what reason. {Nice to meet y'all!} I write for three other blogs, too. Oh, my.

Liz signed a letter of intent to swim for a Colorado college while juggling the demands of choir and club swimming.

Clark has taken Cross-X debate on his high school's national champion debate team by storm and has his eyes on state, and he was the videographer for the varsity football team.

Susanne plays flute in the honors symphonic band at her magnet performing arts middle school, and she swims at a high level, too.

We're very proud of them. And they're teenagers. So, we battle teenage girl mood swings, the "I want" syndrome, ADHD, getting a straight, truthful answer, social media, and social lives. I'd get in more trouble than I could get out of with the three of them if I gave you the details.

We are just like everybody else and nothing like any of them. And we love it. Feel free to read more sometimes-true tales of our adventures at *http://www.pamelahutchins.com*. Or not and say you did. Whatevs.

Just know that in our corner of the world, t'ings is good, mon, even when they're not.

Merry Christmas and Happy New Year, y'all.

\*\*\*

# THE RIGHT STUFF

Clark has many of the raw materials for great success later in life: brains, looks, a wicked sense of humor, and an amazing creative streak. Plus he is an exceptional written and verbal communicator — and, most importantly, his mother rocks!

But he also has challenges to overcome if he's going to realize his potential. Some of them relate to ADHD, such as organization, attention to detail, and follow-through. Others relate to being a teenage boy, such as organization, attention to detail, and follow-through. And some, it's hard to say. Where does his sneaky nature come from? Why does he have trouble with truth? Why does he refuse to listen or answer the question you ask him? Don't ever ask this kid what two plus two equals, because you'll have a long conversation, and four will never come up.

Likely, these last few traits have roots in the ADHD, but I don't know for sure. All I know is that we do the best we can with what we have, but we don't settle for less than we have to. For instance, I have often considered whether to seek classroom accommodations for Clark. Luckily, we have had 95% success with teachers who willingly accommodated him—as they did the unique traits of any of their students—to the best of their abilities. We kept coming to the conclusion that Clark's symptoms weren't severe enough to remove him from the most "normal" (whatever that is) learning environment possible.

If we ever decide otherwise, though, I wouldn't ask for big changes without going through proper channels; I think that puts too much burden on the teacher. I strongly encourage all parents of kids with ADHD to seek accommodations through your school's formal process if you have the slightest inkling that it is in your child's best interests.

Eric, Edward and I also made the tough decision to allow Clark to fail entire classes in his sophomore year, for the following reasons:

1. Clark's consumption of his medication had finally (FINALLY) become routine and was no longer an impetus to combat or trickery.

2. Up through his freshman year, Clark had a great deal of help, support, and training in organizational skills from his parents and his counselor. In middle school, we made him fill out homework/test/issues sheets every day in every class, and at one point, he also had to have his teachers initial each one. By the end of freshman year, we'd backed off to just asking questions instead of requiring documentation.

3. Our school district has a nifty online system for parents to access their child's grades, so I had Clark's progress reports in real time.

4. Clark had expressed his urgent desire to show us he could succeed independently.

And then he failed health, chemistry, and algebra (twice!) during first semester of his sophomore year.

But we made some changes on the fly, the most notable of which was establishing Clark's full-time residence at our house rather than alternating between here and Edward's. They still hang out as frequently as they can, but only after Clark completes his work to my satisfaction, and if it doesn't disrupt his studies. Clark has stability and a routine now.

We did a pantry sweep and eliminated Liz and Susanne's Pop-Tarts. Clark thiefed them, so out they went, over the girls' voluble protests. I told them to take it up with their brother and suggest to him that he follow the rules in the future, hoping for a little peer pressure. It seemed to help.

For breakfast, Clark tended to grab an English muffin or a bagel with butter and grape jelly, if anything, but at the doc's suggestion, we increased the caloric intake and percentage of protein in his morning meal. I started making him chocolate Muscle Milk shakes with a banana, an ice cream scoop of peanut butter, and two scoops of Blue Bell chocolate ice cream (to make him drink it, and because he had become super skinny). This worked so well to increase his focus and alertness that he added a bagel with cream cheese. It was a glorious cycle: The extra nutrients gave him more energy, so he exerted more mental and physical effort, and his appetite improved in turn. We made sure he carb'ed at night with lots of pasta and rice.

I finally accepted that he has trouble waking up on his own and started waking him up earlier to give him his PED before he showered, dressed, and ate. Wow, getting that Concerta in his system thirty minutes earlier made a big difference in Algebra 2, his first class and his academic Achilles' heel.

After he started taking the Concerta earlier, we were able to enforce an earlier bedtime. Bedtime was 10:30, but he hadn't adhered to it. We started sweeping his room and person for electronics and reading materials at 10:00 and put him in lockdown at 10:30. Before, especially when he was alternating houses, he had a bad habit of reading or playing with his iTouch until the wee hours. Because of the earlier bedtime and the stash of purloined electronics on my bedside table, Clark became more able to rise and shine on time.

Here's a big and unexpected change that helped: Clark has a girlfriend. A very smart girlfriend. To see the change that comes over him when he's around her is stunning. His doctor calls it "synchronizing." Clark slows down and calms down. We can communicate with him more effectively when he is standing beside her than we ever have before. How wild is that? And wonderful! Because we see that he CAN do it.

So the final piece to finding the Right Stuff was learning what motivated Clark, something we could not quite figure out for fifteen years. And it is this: Clark wants to compete in debate, for which he must remain academically eligible and have our permission. He also wants to spend time with and impress a very pretty, very sweet girl who is also in debate. Cue the Hallelujah Chorus. With the key to his motivators, we can do anything!

None of our changes may seem like tectonic plate shifters, but the difference between the boy living upstairs at our house now versus the stressed kid of four months ago is staggering. That boy told me that he failed at everything he did. This boy told me he's going to win state in cross-examination before he graduates.

And I believe him. He's got the Right Stuff.

# MUST LOVE DOGS

---

I wish I could say my son loved and related to animals, but I can't. I read about other kids with neuro-atypicality similar to his who bond with pets, especially ADHD kids, and I am jealous. Clark never has.

When he was seven, we bought a puppy. Theoretically, this was going to be his dog. What a fine, handsome yellow lab puppy he was, too. Cowboy would have loved nothing more than to be Clark's dog, to fetch him sticks, to play chase, to splash in the mud together. Except Clark had no interest in the real live animal. All his energy and excitement about getting the puppy lasted for about three minutes. It wasn't that Cowboy disappointed him, hurt him, or scared him. He just didn't measure up to being the most exciting thing in Clark's very narrow frame of reference. Cowboy couldn't outshine a book or a computer game, for instance. So the dog moved on to Clark's five-year old, neuro-typical sister Susanne, who adored him. They remain best friends 'til this day.

When Clark was ten, we got a cat. We thought that possibly a lower maintenance animal that could curl up with him when he was involved in a sedentary pursuit would give him a creature he could relate to. No such luck. Juliet also became Susanne's.

Over the years, we added fish, a guinea pig, a live pig, five more dogs, and another cat. Like with any child, we had to beg him to take care of them. Unlike with our other four kids, though, no animal got through to him. No animal ever rose to "the most important thing in my four seconds-left-to-live" worldview. The animals shouldn't feel too bad about that, though, because most people didn't rise to that level either. We knew he loved us, I knew I was the central figure in his life, but that didn't mean he needed to talk to us, unless required. Clark was not an interacter. He wasn't asocial. He just didn't know how to engage, or really care to, other than, well, theoretically. He floated around the fringe.

Eventually, in his mid-teens, Clark started maturing enough that the worst of his social inabilities passed. He was still the odd kid that might say the extremely unfunny and awkward comment, loudly, but he found a niche with people that "got" him, at the same time as his assertiveness grew.

That's when we got Petey. Petey is a Boston Terrier. When he first came home with us, he was barely over six pounds. Petey was terrified of Clark, and Clark was only mildly interested in Petey, certainly not interested enough to try to figure out how to engage with the small creature. By then, Clark was nearly 16.

Cowboy was jealous of Petey, even more so because Susanne was infatuated with the new puppy. One morning, little Petey got between Cowboy and his food. Petey's cries were heart-wrenching. I ran and scooped him up, only to discover that Cowboy had somehow knocked Petey's googly left eye right out of its socket. Now I cried along with Petey. Well, that was more than Clark could take.

"BAD DOG," he yelled, sending Cowboy hunkering onto his belly on the ground. Clark dragged Cowboy outside. "Mom, it's going to be OK, calm down." Clark put his very big arm around me and squeezed.

It wasn't OK right away, but, in the end, Clark was right. Petey only needed one eye to become a swaggering dynamo of boundless personality. And he only needed one eye to become Cowboy's best friend. It's a relationship that makes us laugh and, occasionally, shiver in terror.

I'd love to claim that overnight Clark took to Petey and learned how to love him. He didn't. But slowly he did soften up for the funny little creature. It took leaving Petey and Clark alone a few evenings together to cement the relationship, but now Petey jumps up into Clark's lap on the couch, and Clark strokes those always-moving oversized black ears.  Clark can say whatever wacky comment enters his mind. Petey doesn't care. He yawns and snuggles closer. Clark still has no relationship with any of our other animals, but empathy for Petey's pain made it through to Clark's center, just as empathy for my pain over Petey touched Clark's heart. Empathy.

And I realize that is it. That is the key. The most fundamental way Clark relates to others – animal or human – is through empathy. Other people don't always "get" him, and he sure doesn't understand how to fit in with them. He can't even figure out how to play with a normal dog, for goodness sake. But when he feels the pain of another creature he cares about, that's when we see the soft center in Clark as well.

Clark would still rather watch a YouTube video of a dog than watch a real dog, or play a game online with a dog in it than play with Cowboy. We saw him bridge the divide with Petey, though, and it opened a window into his soul for us.

In his core, that boy must love dogs after all.

# ON CHAINSAWS AND OTHER STIMULI

So my long-suffering island-boy-to-Texas-transplant husband convinced me that the perfect retreat for our family would be in a secondhand (or would that be thirdhand?) trailer on a bug- and snake-infested piece of property five miles from Nowheresville, Texas — yeah, for real — much to the chagrin of our kids, especially Clark, who announced that his weekends were 100% booked in Houston with debate, robotics, and a girlfriend.

We had been looking for Texas hill country acreage for quite some time. The conversation between my husband and me about this one went something like this:

Eric: I lahhhhke this one. It has a POND on it.

Me: Stop me if I've said this before: Some cowboy is going to kick your ass and good one of these days for making fun of our accents. And ponds have snakes.

Eric: That pond is nahhhhhhce. I lahhhhhhke that pond.

Me: I like that it is only an hour and a half from your office.

Eric: And it has a real nahhhhhhce pond.

Me: I think you've mentioned that. But I can't camp out there. Too many bugs and snakes. And Africa-hot. Plus there's those bugs and snakes.

Eric: We'll get us a travel-trailer. That'd be nahhhhhhce. You'd lahhhhhhke it.

Me: Forget the cowboy. *I'm* going to kick your ass. And I made a promise to myself years ago—no RVs, no travel trailers. Sheets, running water, A/C, indoor potties, and no trailers.

Eric: You're not being very nahhhhhhce.

(Sounds of scuffle and pummeling, and Clark laughing at seeing his mother beating the crud out of his stepdad.)

Well, of course we acquired the property, which we promptly dubbed Shangri-La. Then we bought the trailer-of-a-redneck's-dreams from a real nahhhhhhce couple even further away from Nowheresville, Texas. It came time for Bubba-mon, Clark, and me to stash the trailer on Shangri-La. Clark's sisters conveniently found ways out of helping. Not that their help was ever much help, anyway.

Surprise, surprise, we had some issues.

First, five minutes before we got there, we came to a low bridge on the shortcut route under which our trailer could not pass. As we turned around to take the long way, Cowboy, our 125-pound freakishly large lab, whimpered once, shot Bubba-mon an apologetic look in the rear view mirror, and unloaded the entire contents of his digestive system out his back end and down the spare tire well of our 2000 Suburban. This is how we discovered, to Clark's eternal horror, that four hours really is Cowboy's limit in the car. Oops, had it been that long?

Second, a mere thirty minutes later, this is how Clark discovered that no matter how logical it seems to him, toilet bowl cleaner is **not** the appropriate thing to use to clean dog diarrhea from your vehicle's carpet. No, we don't always carry toilet bowl cleaner with us. We had stocked up on supplies for our new trailer, which by now we had named the Quacker (because *Mallard* is emblazoned across its front window covering). Luckily, those supplies included alternative cleaners to deal with the vaporized carpet.

Third, as my Bubba-mon pulled downhill on our narrow, winding drive to Shangri-La, he swung wide to avoid planting the Quacker into a tree. This is how we discovered the large tree stump under the skinny bush that he had assumed the Suburban would easily skim over. SCRUNCH, FULL STOP.

Fourth, when Bubba-mon was unable to free the Suburban from its high-center position on the stump (trying techniques such as teeter-tottering forward and backward, lifting, lightening the load, etc.), Clark, after many unhelpful and highly irritating suggestions, came up with one good one. He suggested we use our jack to achieve clearance and then gently pull off and over the jack. This is how we discovered that there was no jack in the Suburban, after all. I'm not going to blame the teenage driver of this Suburban, but, well, there is the issue of custodial possession and responsibility. *If you're reading this, Liz, honey, I love you, and I'm just kidding – now you know Clark's special hell.*

Long story short, Bubba-mon ultimately decided that the stump and Suburban were conjoined at a noncritical area, and he got aggressive with the gas pedal. It worked. He employed his superior trailer-backing skills, and we hid the Quacker in the woods and headed home to Houston. Where we slept like the dead.

Three weekends later, we loaded up the truck and we moved to Beverly . . . Shangri-La that is, big ponds, bugs and snakes (cue banjo music). Of course, we ran into a few *issues*.

Upon entering the trailer, a horrible smell assaulted my princess-and-the-pea-like nose.[13] Since the trailer with its poo tank and contents had sat under the Texas July sun, this was not entirely unexpected. Yet, somehow, it was. Unexpected. And really, really awful.

Me: There's something dead in here, Eric.

Bubba-mon: Turn on the A/C. You've got an overly-sensitive nose. It's probably just musty.


Five minutes passed. Meanwhile, Clark made a tactical error: he flushed our brand-new thirdhand potty. A noxious odor filled the trailer. The LP gas detector went off immediately, screeching out its warning to everyone within a five-mile radius.

Me: (running from trailer with towel over my face, Clark gagging on my heels) OH GOD OH GOD OH GOD OH GOD RUN ERIC RUN IT'S GOING TO BLOW

Bubba-mon:       (running)       (IN       THE       WRONG DIRECTION) What the hell's going on?

Me: I don't know. Clark flushed the potty, it got really stinky, and the alarm went off. I'm afraid we have a propane leak. We have to evacuate.

---

[13] I know, this is not a perfect analogy, but run with me on it.

Bubba-mon: Hmmmmm, but the propane isn't even turned on. (Sticks head foolishly into trailer.) Oh, SHIT. What's that smell? (Turns to me.) OH, shit. That's methane gas. (Reaches over and turns off LP gas detector.)

Me: What do we do?

Bubba-mon: I can fix this, no problem.

(This is a phrase oft-repeated in the adventures of Bubba-mon.)

So, first, this is how we discovered that, despite the instructions on the tank treatment bottles that one dosage takes care of a whole "load," you can't leave *anything* in that tank in the hundred-degree Texas heat for three weeks. We could have driven a Prius to Houston and back on the amount of methane we discharged into that twenty-six-foot trailer. "Whew, do not go in there" from *Ace Ventura: Pet Detective* took on a whole new meaning for us that day.

On that trip, we also discovered that chainsaws, bonfires, and Clark do not mix. Eric cranked up the chainsaw and Clark deserted the fire he had been charged with tending and sprinted off with his hands over his ears. Loud noises. Still problematic for him. Almost immediately, flames walked across the clearing and began to lick at the Quacker's underbelly. Well, maybe that's a(nother) slight exaggeration. But trust me on this one: I lost several years of my life during the event.

Despite all of this, or maybe because of it — I dunno — I will grudgingly admit that Bubba-mon was right: This place is nahhhhhce and I lahhhhhke it. I am head over heels for the Quacker, Shangri-La, and Nowheresville.

It's still growing on Clark.

# I'M A SLOW LEARNER.

It took me many years to realize how successful Clark really is. We measured him by the yardsticks we had been measured by. Did he make A's? Was he a good athlete? Was he a popular friend? By all those measures, Clark failed. Each year of elementary school, he did worse against these criterion. In middle school the downward slope of his performance grid fell off at a steeper angle.

We compared him to ourselves. His father and I had made fantastic grades. Edward was a star athlete and had lifelong friends. I was a distance runner and cheerleader. Clark's grades were terrible. He washed up in lacrosse and football and refused to try other sports, refused any physical activity he could, in fact. By the time he was in middle school, he had not friends whatsoever. Zero. Zip. Nada.

Clark didn't just "fail" at school, he failed at home. He was the kid that never did what he was asked, lied more often than he told the truth, and drove all the rest of us crazy with his odd, repetitive behaviors and awkward comments.

We wrung our hands. We bemoaned his (our) situation. We hung our heads. Was it our parenting? Other people seemed to think so. Why couldn't Clark succeed like we had, and like our other four kids did? Why, why, why?

I finally wised-up when Clark was in high school. I was the one who was failing, but not because I failed to force Clark into a cookie-cutter shape of the All American Boy. I was failing because I still worried that my worth was based on what other people thought of my children, people who knew nothing about me or them. People who knew nothing about Clark or neuro-atypicality.

Shame on me.

I examined my feelings *about* Clark. Was I wringing my hands for him or for me? Honestly, it was both. But Clark wasn't wringing his own hands. Clark was, for the most part, happy being Clark, even though being Clark was harder than being me, or being Liz or Susanne, the two siblings closest in age to him. If he was happy, why couldn't I be? I needed to let my Pollyanna Perfection fantasty ideal go. I had to live in the real world, with my real son. And I asked myself an important question: What in my deepest heart did I want most for all my children?

The answer came easily, and it stung: for them to be happy.

So I put his (terrible) report cards away. I let him drop out of lacrosse first, and then football later. I quit pushing him to invite friends over and let him hang out with us. I listened to the sound of his laugh, pure and real. I quit pressuring him about his grades and school work. I let him breathe. I let him exist.

And I made a list of his successes. It looked like this:

- Clark is the kindest member of our family
- Clark is the happiest person in our family
- Clark learns more and knows more than most other young men his age
- Clark does not care what other people think
- Clark is not fearful
- Clark rebounds and recenters faster than anyone I've ever known

How in my right mind could I not count this child as a success, as more of a success than his angst-filled siblings, even? I would succeed as his parent if I just got out of the way and let him be Clark.

I still want him to navigate through the neuro-typical world painlessly, to make it over its hurdles, to reach his own goals. But if in doing that he gets a few failing grades on his report card and wears his flip flops and holey sweats to school with his shirt on inside out and backwards, smiling and relaxed all the while, who am I to take that away from him? And, left to his own devices, he found his niche in robotics and debate, spaces in which he could succeed on anyone's terms, and he even made a few real friends.

Clark has ADHD. He is an Aspie. He is a genius-boy, creative, brilliant, and aggressive. The popular athletic kids think he's weird. And he couldn't care less.

Neither could I.

# "ERIC IS BEING AN

# ASSHOLE."

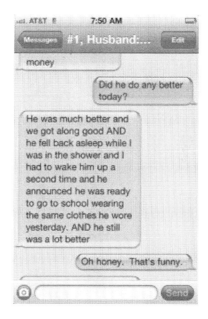

As Clark's parents, Eric and I still count as our *best*
days the types of days other parents read about and

say, "Oh, my kid does that sometimes." Well, our other four do, too, sometimes.

The start of this chapter? An actual text documenting real progress for Clark.

Consider, also, Clark's social and academic progress. He did not have a single friend during middle school. Watching him try to interact with kids his age was like watching Pepé Le Pew, the little skunk from *Looney Tunes*; the kids scattered away from Clark like his odd behaviors were a foul stench.

When he entered high school, he matured just enough to leverage his theatrical flair and his genius IQ with his let's-call-them-quirky behaviors into a niche on the debate team. As a sophomore first-year debater, he blew us all away with his dramatic, aggressive, freaky intelligent, ADHD-infused style. In this, his first year, he missed qualifying for the Texas Forensic Association state tournament with his cross-examination partner by one vote. He even found a **girlfriend** in debate.

Yet, academics and life with Clark continue to challenge us in ways they never do with our four other neuro-typical kids. Sure, they have rare Clark-like days and dish out their own problems, but . . . all four *together* are easier than Clark. So, for example, in the text above, I didn't ask about our two teenage girls, and I didn't edit that part out. They were fine, and I knew it.

Clark is . . . Clark. The hardest issues day by day remain turning in homework, telling the truth, and following instructions. We can't tell whether it is intentional when he promises to put up his clothes when we ask him to, then doesn't do it. All we know, with 100% certainty, is that he will not do it unless we stand and watch until he finishes the task, whereas our other kids will eventually do it 75% of the time when asked. Is this part of the present-orientation — the inability to visualize future consequences for present behavioral choices? Or is it defiance from a kid who knows he can wear us down?

Occasionally, our frustration shows.

So, in the texts below, I'm giving you a 100% unedited look into our life when we get frustrated — the electronic evidence — because it so clearly demonstrates that agony/ecstasy of ADHD parenting, and what our ADHD teenager is like.

First, the backstory: Clark missed state qualification for debate, but his coach invited him to come to the state tournament and watch the team to prep Clark for next year. What an honor! Clark was elated, and pretty much lost his mind with excitement. And then it got worse/better. He missed qualifying for nationals in a different debate event a few weeks later — again, by one vote.

If we thought it was hard to wrestle him down before, oh my, now it was impossible. Our attempts to communicate with him (obtain a straight answer to a question, often repeated multiple times) failed, more often than not. So against this backdrop, I left town for a business trip.

Eric, who is a great and patient stepdad, had to go it alone. And because karma's a bitch, things went south for him, too. He worked late on a project, only to discover as he left at midnight that everything he'd done that day was built upon an error. Twelve hours of redo awaited him the next day.

That morning, Eric tried to wake up Clark. It took three trips upstairs to roust him. While Eric was there, he discovered, AGAIN, all Clark's clean clothes strewn on the floor and the iPad and iTouch contraband on Clark's bed beside him. They were late leaving for school and work. And that's when I heard from THAT BOY.

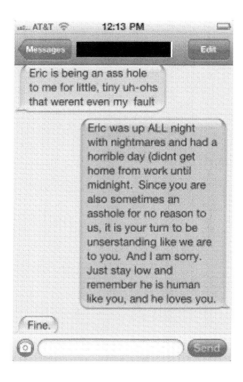

Woopsie. "Eric is being an asshole" is not what I expected. I checked in with Eric and learned the deets. I fired off another to the WonderKid.

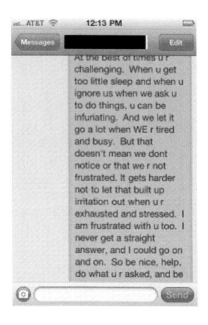

Some of you might not parent just like me and call your kid an asshole back. I can embrace that. But my blunt reply worked with Clark. If I'd yelled at him for calling Eric an asshole, I wouldn't have had his attention. Instead, I spoke his language.

And can I just admit that, while it wasn't funny to either Eric or me, I had a little giggle from the safety of my hotel? In our blended family, we treasure honesty and dropped barriers. I thought it was pretty healthy that Eric and Clark were able to have a morning like this, then make up and move on.

Still, I don't minimize what Eric was going through that morning, because most days it is me.

Which makes Mom the asshole, too.

# EVERYONE BLAMES THE MOTHER.

Do you ever feel like no one out there understands what it's like to parent a neuro-atypical child? I do.

Even the people closest to me haven't always seemed to get it. My husband does now, but he didn't used to. Not until he'd lived with us for a year as Clark's stepdad did he finally accept that he could not do by strength of will and caring what we had not been able to do for Clark before, which is make him "mainstream." He truly believed that with him supporting me, we could get Clark to turn in homework, make friends, and tell the truth. Now Eric gets it, and he helps tremendously, but he can't fix it.

My friends don't. "Have you tried _____?" they ask me. "It sounds like he needs accountability and organizational skills."

*Sigh*

Tell me truly: Have any of you ever been given advice about how to "fix" your ADHD child that had *any* impact — let alone truly worked? I suspect there are very few raised hands out there.

My parents didn't. When Clark was fourteen, they asked me to let him move in with them. I know they didn't mean to suggest I was failing as a parent, but let's just say that they believed it was in his best interests to let them have a try. I declined gently. I said, "Thank you for offering." Inside, I cried my eyes out.

What was I doing wrong this time? What did even my parents believe they could fix that I couldn't? It wasn't (and isn't) that I am angry with my loved ones. I appreciate that they care. After a while, though, my teeth wear down from gritting, and my jaw gets sore from clenching.

So it is with a poignant sense of relief and (yes) vindication that I tell you about a short conversation I had recently with my mother.

"I wanted you to know that the reason your dad and I asked you to let Clark live with us was because we live in a small town where all the kids have more opportunity to participate and shine. We thought if Clark just experienced one small success, at anything, that everything would turn around for him. That if he could build off a success, he would find motivation to succeed at many more things," she said.

I stared at her over the top of my Starbucks venti skinny cinnamon dolce latte, tightening my stomach in anticipation of what was coming next, ready to paste on a smile, bite my lip, and make anything she said OK.

"We were wrong, and I'm sorry," my mother said.

My abdomen unclenched. This was not what I had expected. "Thank you, Mom, thank you very much, that means a lot to me."

"We realize he had some big successes this year in debate and socially, but that didn't change a thing about how he thinks or operates."

My words came out in a rush. "He doesn't need to be like us, Mom. He's a lovable little sucker just as he is. All six feet of him. We don't need to fix him, we just need to help him survive growing up in a world where the rules for success are set by and for people like us."

"And pray he has a great personal assistant some day," she said, and reached across the table to pat my hand, enjoying our shared and oft-repeated memory of his third grade teacher's words.

Amen.

And thanks, Mom. I love you.

# THANK YOU, OLD SPICE

Does your ADHD child struggle with hygiene? Does he forget to brush his teeth for days on end unless you stand and watch him? Does she need the aid of a cattle prod to get her into the shower? If so, I'm sure you have experienced some moments of . . . frustration . . . over personal cleanliness.

At our house, the (complete lack of) hygiene habits of Clark merely caused teeth-grinding until he turned thirteen. Truth be told, all of our kids hated soap, water, and toothpaste. Susanne's stinky feet were legendary; Liz's hair was in dreadlocks for three years because she refused to brush it. But the neuro-typical kids' issues resolved themselves naturally, when they hit puberty.

Clark hit thirteen and nothing changed. Well, nothing changed in terms of his absolute inability to remember that each and every morning of his life he was to use deodorant, wash his face, and brush his teeth. That stayed the same.

Our morning conversations before leaving for school still sounded like this:

"I'm ready to go," Clark would say.

"Have you brushed your teeth?" I would ask in reply.

"Uh, no."

"Please go back upstairs and brush your teeth and take care of *all* your personal hygiene needs."

Five minutes later . . .

"I'm ready to go," Clark would announce.

"Did you put on deodorant?" I would ask.

"Uh, no."

"Go back upstairs, again, and put on deodorant and TAKE CARE OF *ALL* YOUR PERSONAL HYGIENE NEEDS."

Five minutes later . . .

"I'm ready to go," Clark would proclaim.

"NOT IF YOU HAVEN'T WASHED YOUR FACE. TELL ME YOU WASHED YOUR FACE. PLEASE, DID YOU WASH YOUR FACE?"

"Uh . . ."

We always try very hard to help, but we do not do all the thinking for him, despite how much more challenging it makes our lives. *Thank you, years of counseling.* We kept a morning checklist in his room, but by middle school, it was just part of the wallpaper.

Anyway . . .

So now, Clark was in middle school, he was thirteen, and his hormones had kicked in. By telling you that his hormones had kicked in, you might think I mean that he had developed an interest in girls. Why, yes, he had. But what I'm really telling you is that he had started to smell like rotten beef within five minutes of showering sans application of mass quantities of extra-strength deodorant. He smelled so bad that sometimes I had to roll down the car window and stick my head outside to keep from gagging. Really.

The unique odor of stinky teenage boy is well known to all parents of pubescent males. Our older son smelled worse during puberty, but it wasn't usually an issue because he didn't want to smell bad around girls. He showered, used deodorant, and heaped on cheap cologne. He was neuro-typical.

However, with our ADHD son, from the ages of thirteen to fifteen, the problem was chronic, daily, and life-altering. If we weren't standing outside the bathroom door as he exited the shower, then we could not stop the inevitable impact those hormones would have on all of us. Poor kid? Poor Mom! Many are the times I sent him back to the shower for a do-over.

It's hard to advise parents of teenagers similar to mine how to cope with this issue. We had Old Spice Pro Strength stashed in every room of the house for emergency applications. That didn't even work all the time. He had a girlfriend, but she didn't seem to provide the bump he needed, either. I don't know how the poor girl was able to stand it, bless her beautiful heart.

The good news is that they grow out of it. Clark hit sixteen and the stench abated. Not because of markedly better hygiene—although it is *marginally* better as he matures and remembers his meds—but because the worst of the hormones are behind him.

So my best advice, other than shipping them to a year-round cold weather climate? Purchase a gas mask, and know that this too shall pass.

# ROAD DAZE

Let's see . . .

- He processes about half the signals he receives . . .
- He forgets to tell me most of what his plans are . . .
- He is prone to sudden, impulsive changes of direction when *walking* . . .
- He substitutes his own judgment for rules and adult guidance . . .
- He's a MALE . . .
- He's obsessed with technology, dials, gadgets, and gizmos . . .

And he wants us to let him get a driver's license??? Lord help us all.

When our middle child Liz turned fifteen, we sponsored her to obtain a hardship license so she could drive to and from school, swim practice, and her job teaching swimming lessons. It made sense. She's über-responsible, and both Eric and I travelled unpredictably for work. She accelerated and braked too fast, but other than that, we were as comfortable as we could get with the concept of her driving. And she did fine.

Kids are all different. We would no more have handed Clark a set of keys on his fifteenth birthday than given him a switchblade and suggested he play tiddlywinks with it. But the occasion of his fifteenth birthday did make us pause to think: his sixteenth birthday cometh. His grandparents have an old Tahoe with his name on it. What shall we do?

One option was to hold off indefinitely until he was older. Much older. However, we decided to keep that one in abeyance, in case of dishonesty. Instead, we planned this approach:

1. Have his doctor sternly lecture him on ADHD, meds, and driving: *Thou shalt consume all meds or thou shalt not drive.* She's already has this convo with him once. We will facilitate a re-chat. If he misses meds, he can't drive.

2. He will attend the legally mandated drivers' ed program and spend the summer driving with a parent in the front passenger seat for further evaluation and potential veto.

3. We will allow him to drive only to school and back or on pre-approved short trips. He will take his younger sister to school each day. I once put Clark in charge of negotiating a plane change on the way to visit their grandparents. Eleven-year-old Susanne ultimately had to have him paged at the airport when it was time to board and he was nowhere to be found; he was reading a gaming magazine at a newsstand and he'd lost his boarding pass. Susanne saved him. We're hoping she will stabilize the home-school commute as well — and tattle.

4. We are considering the installation of a GPS system in the car that will alert us if he strays from the planned pathways or breaks other driving laws (family or state). He loses driving privileges immediately if this occurs.

5. We are researching phone-jamming options.

The top cause of death for teens is auto accidents, and ADHD teens are at an even higher risk. Some of our rules make sense for non-ADHD teens; other teens don't need quite this level of hovering. Clark has ADHD, and me for a mom. He needs it.

We got lucky: ADHD ruled the timeline for Clark's license. When it was time to let him take driver's education, he needed a verification of enrollment from his high school in order to obtain his learner's permit from the Department of Public Safety.

Guess how long it took for him to remember to get the VOE—even with daily reminders face to face and by text, phone, and email? Two months. He wasn't eligible for his license until six months after he got his learner's permit, so this moved the whole timeline in the right direction.

When he finally reached the magic date to get his license, I asked him to fill out one of the required forms.

"We'll go on Wednesday. Have the form ready for my signature," I reminded him three times.

"Uh huh," he said.

Guess how long it took him to fill out the form? Two weeks.

Once he'd finally filled out the form, I asked him to gather up his learner's permit, birth certificate and Social Security card. This is when he discovered that he had lost the Social Security card when filling out job applications the previous summer.

Guess how long it took to get the Social Security card replaced? Three weeks.

By this time, it was past Thanksgiving, and all his busy parental units said, "Sorry, dude. After the holidays."

Total time added to sixteenth birthday? Five months.

And counting.

Yay!

# HOLDING OUR BREATH

Every year of my kids' lives, I struggle to know how much to hold on, and how much to let go. I see them slipping through my fingers even as I'm sure they feel like my hands are clutched around their throats, each of them straining for a breath of freedom. As they make their way up through elementary, middle and high school, and then on to college, my husband and I have unique worries for each of them.

And then there's Clark. With him, it is worry to the power of ten. Worry to the nth degree. Worry infinity. He is our Formula One race car brain with faulty Geo Prism brakes, headed for a crash. We worry . . .

- Will he (ever) turn in his homework?
- Will that brilliant mind slow down enough to do pre-calc?

- Can I get him to take his online SAT course, or is the lure of other screens too great?
- If he only cares about NOW, how do I know he has appreciation for the dangers? Alcohol? Drugs? Sex/disease/pregnancy?
- You mean the DPS licensed THAT BOY to drive a car? Are they CRAZY?
- If one of us doesn't do a bed check at midnight, will he sleep?
- Will CPS come get him if I can't make him shower all week?
- Can he handle the disappointment of not getting into the college he dreams of because his GPA was dragged down by all that missed homework?
- Who's going to pry him away from screens, out of his room, and into class at college? (And will they be able to make him shower?!?)

This list has been shortened for this chapter, I assure you.

So, taking just the here and now into consideration for a moment, my son has begged us for years to ease our oversight of his schoolwork. How easy it is to say yes and accept a respite from the grind, but how hard it is for the lifeguard in me to let him flail and gasp for breath in the deep end. We'd made a step-change decrease in oversight when he was a sophomore, and he narrowly escaped summer school in two subjects. Now he wanted more freedom. His first week grades—which I check online—included a missed homework and a failed quiz. The old me would have gone through his backpack and Trapper Keeper, emailed the teacher, and required Clark to show me a daily list of assignments, then check in with me as he completed each one.

His psychiatrist and counselor each offered me the same opinion, though: He needs to grow up to be an adult, independent of his parents, and he needs to start now. Let him decide what his goals are and how to achieve them. Loosen the grip, Mom. Decrease the monitoring. Let him learn from the natural consequences of his actions. Step in if it's health or safety; otherwise, let him use some of the skills we all worked on with him over the years, but in his own way. Even if it means he fails.

*Breathe, Pamela, breathe.*

So my son and I talked about his goals for his junior year. Clark said his goals were to turn in homework, make As and Bs, excel in debate, and kill the SAT.

I asked him how he planned to achieve those goals.

He stared at me blankly.

I asked again, and I saw he was starting to shake his head.

I gave an inch, engaging in the negotiation method we had learned to use. "How about I trust you, and I only step in if you need help?"

"If I ASK for help," he said.

"If you start failing classes," I insisted.

"OK, but I want to do this on my own."

He wants to do it on his own, he wants everyone to quit trying to control him, I know he does, but the reality of those failed grades in week one mocked my intentions.

In the end, all the stars were aligned for me to ease up. Clark was taking his meds. He was showing a normal amount of teenage angst, anger, and rebellion, but nothing troubling, and he had reasonable explanations for his non-performance: He had spent too much time prepping for debate (he reached semi-finals in his first tournament, yay!), which was intensive the first few weeks of school, but would then get easier.

Well, he *had* worked on debate until midnight each night. So we settled on a temporary "No girlfriend over while you're doing homework until your grades are all passing" rule, and agreed that he would do homework and SAT prep before his obsession, debate.

Negotiation complete.

It appears there is no precision test to determine how much to let go, and when. But my fingermarks are receding from his neck.

# Shut Up, Clark

For every "negative" trait associated with ADHD, there is a corresponding trait of awesomeness. It is often the same with my son Clark's co-morbid condition, Asperger's Syndrome.

His positives come to mind quickly: He is creative, passionate, and funny.

The negatives aren't hard to remember either. He is unfocused, distracted, relentless, at times insensitive, and always impulsive.

The distractibility can drive us to, well, distraction. But we laugh about it. One time, Liz and Susanne made t-shirts for all of us to wear with Clark's picture on it, captioned with "Huh?" and "What?" Yep, that's it, at the top of this chapter. Distracted. Definitely.

Another time, as we rode the Maid of the Mist at Niagara Falls, the boat captain advised us that if we saw anything out of the ordinary, we should report it to the crew.

"Should we tell them about Clark?" I teased.

"Huh?" Clark asked.

See how the negative can turn positive at times? Go Mom, getting away with that little comment.

Clark is funny. He is very funny . . . sometimes. By the sheer number of impulsive swings he takes at the ball, he is bound to connect at least sometimes. By the will of his relentless pounding, he occasionally scores a homerun.

"What do you want to do tonight, Daniel? I want to go see Harry Potter and the Butt of the Monkeys," he announced to the thin air one day. This made no sense, but left his sisters laughing helplessly for days every time he repeated it. And repeated it. And repeated it. But so did the girls.

More Clarkisms:

"I like cheese." (Repeated 7,000 times a day for three years)

"I'm a dog." (Repeated 5,000 times a day for two years)

Often he misses the ball by a mile, leaving us befuddled, bemused, or even uncomfortable at his unfunniness. Sometimes even wounded. Like when he blurted out, "Why can't we talk about our summer

vacation in front of Liz?" right in front of Liz when we
had told him that she couldn't go with us on vacation
because she'd be visiting her mother. He is sweet, he
doesn't want to hurt any feelings, but he is missing the
social savvy and empathy genes.

Take the issue of race, for instance. Clark is very comfortable with the race issue, and he finds great humor in
it. Meanwhile, I am an employment lawyer and human
resources consultant. I live in terror of his casual comments. Like when he was playing Scattergories with his
girlfriend and her parents and sisters. His girlfriend is
Black, or Blasian, as she describes herself on her Facebook profile—her father is African American and her
mother is Filipino. Clark could not look more Caucasian.
As an answer to "Things that are black" beginning with
the letter F, Clark's answer was "the Fosters." Yes, their
family name is Foster. Luckily, they all thought he was
hilarious.

He is missing a good set of antilock brakes on his
brain and mouth. When he gets the urge to speak, when
he feels the need to indulge his own funny bone, absolutely nothing will stop him.

Nothing.

"It doesn't get any funnier if you say it ten times,
Clark," I advise him.

"Shut up, Clark," his sisters shout.

"We dropped that subject an hour ago. Let it go," Eric counsels him.

He is passionate about football. He is obsessed with football. Not *playing* football—just strategizing about football and watching it. And talking about it. Endlessly. This makes him a lot like many other guys, while totally different from them at the same time. My husband and his oldest son have a love for football. They both played football for years. Yet Clark's questions about historic football minutiae and obscure facts about current practice squad pro players, posed as hypotheticals with seventy-three follow-up questions, floor even them.

I started this chapter, though, talking about the positives. Clark's worst ADHD/Asperger's traits are positives to him. They transcend their "disorder" labels, especially when he is regularly taking his meds, which enable him to SLOOOWWW DOOOWWWNNN and utilize some of the skills he has (sort of) learned, especially after he hit the magical age of sixteen and his symptoms started to subside slightly.

If you turn Clark loose on a topic in which he has an interest, then you had better stand back and hold on to your bum with both hands, because he's about to rocket-launch you into lunar orbit. Aside from football, he also loves public policy, he laps up computer science, he devours world history, he churns through words, he lives for games. Don't expect him to waste his time on grammar, pre-calculus, or chemistry, but if you want to see a protostar, a dark nebula extraordinaire, shout, "Resolved: The United States federal government should substantially increase its exploration and/or development of space beyond the Earth's mesosphere," and assign him the affirmative case. He will laser-focus. He will employ all of that creativity and passion as he relentlessly, and, yes, insensitively, pounds you with his arguments, sometimes forcefully pushing the first point that enters his mind, rather than the best one. His girlfriend, who also is a cross-examination debater, would add that he will scare you.

You will forget about his "disabilities." You will marvel at his amazing abilities, and you will want to shout, "Shut UP, Clark," out of intimidation.

But you probably won't.

You might cheer or pump your fist, however, instead. "Go, Clark!" you might yell. Meanwhile, I am whispering in his ear.

"Please, Clark, please, remember: Never, ever, *ever* let anyone shut you up."

# ABC, 123, SAT, Baby You and Me

It's that time.

Time for me to stress about Clark's fast-approaching adulthood. Time for me to think about the impact of his less-than-stellar high school grades on his college applications. Time for me to worry about keeping him focused through SAT prep or over the course of a half-day exam.

Shoot me now!

Clark, however, assures me all this fuss is for naught. He's gonna ace it.

He always says that. Right after he learns he has an F going into the final because he has missed too many homeworks. The problem is that he always HAS aced it before, whatever "it" was. He has passed classes by making near-perfect scores on his finals five times in his two and a half years of high school.

You read that right. Five times.

No amount of counter-information from me convinces him the SAT won't be more of the same. He is predictably and stunningly overconfident that he doesn't need the online prep course. Ah, how ADHD of him. And how terrifying.

I look at my man-child, the whisper of moustache on the once baby-smooth face, the size-eleven feet that used to wear Dallas Cowboys booties. Only his Bambi eyes remain the same. I've never convinced him of anything before, but this time, I have ammunition. I have carrots.

A girl. Debate club competitions. And avoidance of taking the live SAT prep class.

Aha! Clark agreed to working through CollegeBoard's online prep class for half an hour each day before he can spend time with his girlfriend or work on debate. He has to finish his homework first, too. All of this with the TV off, after a {gigantic} snack and a minimum of Facebook. I have to pace behind him every few minutes to police this last requirement.

Then, he can take the test once. No accommodations, no live prep class. If he kills it, he's done. If he doesn't score at a level that helps him accomplish his stated college goals, then it is on to live class and possible accommodations.

His goal is, at a minimum, to get into the University of North Texas so he can participate in their debate program. It is one of the few of its kind in Texas. His stretch goal is to gain admission to the University of Texas at Austin, which has the same type of debate team, or Texas A&M University which he has loved all his life. He believes his stretch goal is possible. We try to hide our skepticism. We are just happy (very happy) that he has found an attainable school that he likes, and that it prides itself on its success rate with ADHD students.

Clark's pre-Advanced Placement English teacher recommends that all kids, especially those with disability issues benefited by maturity, take the SAT no earlier than March of their junior year. Boy, do I feel bad for our first three kids now. They all took it the fall of their junior year. According to his teacher, every bit of maturity aids in focusing during the long four-hour test. This makes perfect sense to me. She also told me that she and his other teachers would not finish teaching the topics included on the SAT until then. I was sold.

So, preparations continue, and will continue, for months. If we need to, we can request SAT or ACT test accommodations, which can include individual administration of the test; computerized, audio, or large-print test editions; and extended testing time. We'll see in March.

Which leaves me with a lot of time to monitor Facebook usage.

# COLLEGE WON'T KILL US, BUT IT FEELS LIKE IT WILL.

---

Remember way back thousands of words ago when I wrote that Clark skipped kindergarten before we knew he had ADHD? The well-intentioned suggestion from his private school and our misguided decision about it have haunted us ever since.

Especially now, when we are staring down the barrel at graduation.

"Come on, frontal lobe. Develop. Develop," I urge. "You can do it, Clark, practice those life skills. Just once, to show you were listening. Go, boy, go!"

We've had seventeen years to help him, and the time has come to guide him in choices that may take him outside the reach of our immediate assistance. One might think this process of choosing his path would be long and twisting.

One would be wrong.

Clark knows himself like none of our other four kids do.

"Why don't you take a year off to work and travel first?" his dad suggested, angling for an extra year of maturity to offset the ADHD/Asperger's.

"Why don't you pick a college in Houston or near your grandparents?" I threw out.

"What about Blinn? It's a Texas A&M feeder," Eric tried. Clark had loved Texas A&M all his life.

No.

No.

No.

All our great suggestions met Clark's stone wall.

"I am going to do Cross-X debate in college. There are two schools in Texas with the right type of debate teams: University of Texas and University of North Texas," Clark informed us.

He knew he had to choose among the public Texas universities or foot the difference in cost himself, by scholarship, loan, or job. He was opting for the route that cost him no extra. Smart boy.

Forget for a moment the mind-blowing significance of choosing UT over Texas A&M, its archrival and my alma mater. Unfortunately for Clark, Texas's public universities offer automatic acceptance to every Texas high school student who finishes in the top 10% of his or her class. This top 10% fills nearly the entire entering class for universities of top choice like Texas A&M and the University of Texas at Austin. Clark attended a prestigious public high school well-known for its tough curriculum and students' high academic performance. His 3.4+ GPA would place him well below the top 10%. Even a perfect SAT or ACT score might not get him into UT.

"I want to go to UT," he continued.

Not only were his chances of getting into UT slim to none, but his chances of achieving academic success there were not great, either. At fifty thousand students, UT is one of the largest universities in the United States. In the world, even. It's very easy for an above-average student to get lost in the crowd. It's terrifying to think of a young person like Clark in that environment. UT is not well-known for its friendliness to learning disabilities, either.

Not that Clark would avail himself of their services. He furiously rejects accommodations and takes medication under duress. UNT, on the other hand, while also large, has a better reputation within the Learning Disabled (LD) community. And Clark's grades would meet their admission requirements, especially with a decent

SAT score. As far as Texas schools go, Texas Tech University comes highly recommended for its Techniques program for students with ADHD and other disabilities, but its debate program didn't meet Clark's criterion.[14]

We set up an appointment for Clark with his high school counselor, hoping he would listen to a realistic adult viewpoint.

"The counselor said I have to raise my grades, but that she has seen kids with worse grades than me get admitted to UT," he announced after the meeting.

Talk about selective hearing. I had spoken with the counselor, too, and knew this was a gross misrepresentation of her overall message.

So be it. We would not change Clark's mind. I might change his perspective, however.

Thus began my campaign to elevate UNT from his fallback school to an accepted lead candidate, with UT as a stretch goal for an upperclass transfer. My reasoning is that either Clark will entrench himself at UNT and stay,

---

[14] There are some great books with advice on colleges for students with special needs, and I've cited a few in the Resources chapter.

or that he will mature enough to weather the transfer to UT when he is twenty instead of eighteen.

As we traverse our last year before Clark chooses a college, we are focusing on teaching him the skills that will help him overcome his poor executive function and succeed at college. At least once a week, we require him to get himself up and running without assistance. If he fails to do so, he forfeits time with his girlfriend. We have started assigning him tasks to complete before school to keep him from sitting down at his laptop for a little early morning Facebook chatting. We've developed higher expectations about how he uses his study time.

It's a big elephant. We take little bites, one at a time.

I still close my eyes and see a bleary-eyed boy in soiled clothes sitting between towers of pizza boxes with a Playstation controller in his hand, his schoolbooks unopened behind him on the kitchen table. But I see him in UNT Eagle-green now, and it looks good on him.

Now I just have to hire someone to cattle-prod Clark out of bed and hand him his PED each morning.

# IT IS LOVE, ACTUALLY.

Love. Love. Love.

It's all we need right? Well, sort of. Theoretically. Love looks and feels differently, to some people, though. Take Clark, for example. He thinks about love. He even has love, or something like it. He has dated the same sweet neuro-typical girl for over a year.

But the form love takes when practiced by an ADHD teen doesn't look like the love I, as a non-ADHD person, remember feeling, or that I do feel for my gorgeous husband Eric even now. To me, young love is urgent. It is all-consuming. It makes you do crazy things. Operative word? DO. As in "take action."

That's where my son differs so much from my experience. Clark is completely happy in his four-second window of life; the past is gone, the future doesn't exist. Anything that enters that window and stays with him is awesome. But if it's not there, then he really doesn't miss it all that much. Maybe a little. If his girlfriend texts him and asks him to miss it, for instance. As in, if she texts and says, "Look, here I am, and I'm not with you." Then he misses it. He continues playing FIFA Soccer on the Xbox with a smile on his face, but he kinda sorta misses her. Things might be even better if she were here. She's not though. And he's still happy. He doesn't need to DO anything. It's all good.

Sometimes they ride to school together. Her sister drops her at our house before 7:00 a.m. Eric and I aren't always dressed and out of the bathroom yet at this time. She rings the doorbell in the dark. *Surely Clark is up and will answer*, I think. *Surely he knows when she was due to arrive*. The doorbell keeps ringing. She weighs 90 pounds sopping wet, and I can't take it any longer. I sprint to the door in my half-tied robe and let her in.

"I'm sorry. He's not awake. I'll get him," I apologize. She and I have had this exchange before. We have it most days.

She settles in happily, making strawberry icing doo-dle-art on the toaster strudels. I stomp up the stairs where two alarm clocks blare over Clark's snore.

"Wake up."

It takes three tries, but he does, finally.

"Shower, take your pill, get downstairs. You promised to wake up in time to let her in. You left her standing in the dark again."

Grunts tell me he hears me, and I stomp back down the stairs.

Later that night, Eric and I ask each other, "What kind of love is it when a boy -- a young man -- leaves his girlfriend outside in the cold, in the dark, day after day?"

I know what kind. It's the feeling of love, the emotion of love, but without the urgency of the future consequences to the lovers. It's the kind of love that doesn't anticipate the stranger with the knife in the bushes watching the girl. It's the kind of love that doesn't see the new boy next year who would never leave her standing alone in the dark. It can't imagine how much a broken heart will hurt. For awhile.

I've had this love before. Clark's father. It didn't last. I needed the action of love. I needed a love that remembered I hurt when I wasn't screaming. That everything wasn't OK just because the crisis fell outside the four-second window.

I sat across the table recently from a man in between Clark's age and the age of Edward. The young man had just told me had ADD. He had questions.

"It's so hard," he explained. "Relationships, I mean. I don't do them very well."

I thought of Edward, and the love that withered, the problems left unresolved, the attentions not paid, the actions not taken, the things said that fell outside his focus. The challenges he had that were too much for me. I thought of Clark, and the years ahead. The beautiful young girl in the dark on the front porch.

My heart aches. I've worried about this for a long time. Like I've worried about homework, grades, his previous lack of friends, wrecked cars, and drugs. In the same way as I worry someday that his Asperger's will assert itself at work in the form of an unfiltered and outside the lines comment that seems totally appropriate to him, and costs him a job he loves, or at least needs.

I've worried about how to teach him that the feeling of love feeds on the acts of love, which are spurred by the future of love. Future. The future he doesn't quite anticipate.

Love. Love. Love.

I love this boy. I love him enough to let him find his own path, my voice as I try to explain in a way he'll understand hopefully echoing in his head. "Love, showing love, means you make her the emergency. Love is urgent." He doesn't understand now. He doesn't need to yet. Maybe if he's lucky, he'll find someone who understands him and doesn't need anything more than he gives.

Surely, a heart as kind and loving as his doesn't need to be broken. So, I pray.

# THE NOT-SO-FAR OFF AND NOT-SO-DISTANT FUTURE

You're nearing the end of my chronicle of the adventures of Clark Kent. Maybe, like me, you feel a twinge of regret or even sadness that the journey is almost over. The parenting journey, that is. Clark's journey will continue long after we break the champagne bottle over the hull of his adulthood and shout "Bon voyage."

And that's what our whole job as parents was aimed toward, right? To prepare these marvelous creatures, these gifts from God, for their independence day? To create the greatest possibility that they will live a productive, accountable life, able to pursue their own happiness?

So, what does this look like for our children, the future adults of ADHD (or ADHD and a host of co-morbid challenges)? Can they, do they, create lives of happiness and productivity?

234

Most of us have an older model to compare to. Remember, ADHD is largely genetic. Who in your family carries the ADHD mantle ahead of your child? Their successes and challenges may foreshadow the issues your child will face.

For Clark, we turn to his father. Edward was undiagnosed as a child, but his natural intelligence and a very strong mother kept him organized and high-performing through high school. His struggles started in college. The first college tip for ADHD kids is to seek help, but the undiagnosed don't have a name for their problems, so they don't know where to turn. Often, they self-medicate with drugs or alcohol. The diagnosed have it a little easier.

As an adult, Edward sought his opposite in a partner, a woman with extremely developed executive skills that compensated for his own. Moi. He showed a wonderful resilience and ability to let go of the past and not worry about the future. On the other hand, he showed an irritating and frustrating (to me) inability to remember the past and plan for the future. He found consistency in parenting extremely difficult. He suffered from anxiety attacks and insomnia. Even so, his issues did not prevent him from achieving success in his career. He had to work much harder at focus, organization, and time management than his peers, but his creativity and enthusiasm made up for it.

Beyond the Edward in your family tree, there is a wealth of information available on adult ADHD at our fingertips on the internet. One of my favorite blogs from an adult with ADHD is *Mungo's ADHD*[15]. The author speaks candidly about overcoming ADHD's limitations while celebrating and benefitting from its wonderful positive traits.

When I speak to ADHD adults, I commonly hear sadness that things are so hard and that their condition hampers their performance. Yet from my own headcount within my survey group, the most common denominator seems to be a parental reluctance to seek diagnosis and treatment when they were younger. I think this factor, while anecdotal, is critical. If you are an ADHD adult, first, HUGS to you. Second, please flip to the Resources chapter for a list of wonderful resources on and for adult ADHD. I am thrilled and hopeful about the growing community — both online and off — of parents, kids, and adults dealing with ADHD. Together, we are breaking the cycle of ignorance and stigmatism.

I can't chronicle Clark's future until it is the past. But after seventeen years of living with this amazing boy —

---

[15] http://www.mungosadhd.com

this whacker of cactuses, wearer of lacrosse gloves, saboteur of lawnmowers, this cape-wearing WonderKid—I can predict with confidence that the positives will compensate for the negatives, and that he is ready for the journey, his steamer trunk packed and his passage booked.

Bon voyage, Clark.

I love you, kid.

# RESOURCES

God has an incredible sense of humor. He gave me, the ultra-type-A slightly-OCD mom, an ADHD child to nurture to adulthood. Somehow, Clark will survive me; I have faith. Somehow I will survive him; I am tough.

It won't be for lack of help and resources, though, and I want to share some of my favorites with you. Maybe you picked up a few good ideas along the way as you read *The Clark Kent Chronicles*, but I touched only the issues that impacted both Clark and me. All kids are different, even (and especially) kids on the ADHD spectrum. Maybe the issues you need help with weren't addressed. If not, I hope you find the sources you need here.

### General Information:
- http://www.drhallowell.com/add-adhd/ (Amazingly positive doctor/author)

- http://www.drhallowell.com/blog/ (Dr. Hallowell's blog)
- http://www.additudemagazine.com (The Bomb)
- http//www.pediatricneurology.com (Dr. Martin Kutscher)
- http://www.chadd.org (Children and Adults with ADHD)

## Community/Support:
- http://adhdmomma.com (Love! {a mom's view of ADHD})
- http://easytolovebut.com (Also love – Easy to Love but Hard to Raise)
- http://special-ism.com
- http://everydayhealth.com

## Accommodations/IEP/504:
- http://www.wrightslaw.com/ (Assistance and advocay)
- http://helpguide.org/mental/adhd_add_t eaching_strategies.htm (Helping ADHD kids succeed)
- http://www.additudemag.com/adhd/artic le/1664.html (Accommodations)

- http://pediatricneurology.com/schoolrx.ht m (Schoolwork and ADHD)
- http://www.additudemag.com/adhd/artic le/711.html (Accomodations)
- http://www.additudemag.com/adhd/artic le/6259.html (IEP meetings)
- http://www.additudemag.com/adhd/artic le/782.html (Meetings with schools)

**<u>Teens:</u>**
- ADHD teens are at an even higher risk: http://erikalynsmith.suite101.com/adhd-teens-face-high-risk-of-injury-or-death-in-auto-accidents-a310936
- GPS system in the car: http://www.mobileteengps.com and http://www.tracktecndriver.com
- Phone jamming for driver usage: http://www.networkworld.com/communi ty/node/36272
- How can parents best help treat their ADHD teens? On diagnosing and treatment for ADD/ADHD teen behavior challenges and symptoms.

- by Peter Jaksa, Ph.D.,
  http://www.additudemag.com/adhd/artic
  le/720.html

**The College Years:**
- Look for pages like these on college websites:
  - http://www.unt.edu/oda/apply/reqs/
    learning.html
  - http://www.depts.ttu.edu/techniques/
  - http://scs.tamu.edu/LD
  - http://www.utexas.edu/diversity/ddc
    e/ssd/index.php
- http://www.edgefoundation.org/schools/adh
  d-friendly-colleges/ (Coaching and support
  system to mainstream your student in college
  not geared toward ADHD/ADD/LD success)
- http://add.about.com/od/schoolissues/a/Tip
  s-for-College_2.htm (Tips for ADHD college
  students)
- http://www.amazon.com/gp/product/037576
  6332?ie=UTF8&tag=edgefound-
  20&linkCode=as2&camp=1789&creative=39095
  7&creativeASIN=0375766332 (K & W Guide to
  Colleges for Students with Learning
  Disabilities)

- http://www.amazon.com/Survival-Guide-College-Students-ADHD/dp/1591473896/ref=pd_sim_b1 (ADHD survival guide for college)
- http://add.about.com/od/childrenandteens/f/ADHD-College.htm (ADHD college guide)
- http://add.about.com/od/adhdresources/a/Scholarships.htm (Scholarships)
- http://www.additudemag.com/adhd/article/1597.html (SAT and ACT tips)
- http://www.collegeboard.com/ssd/student/ (SAT accommodations)
- http://www.act.org/aap/disab/ (ACT accommodations)
- http://www.additudemag.com/adhd/article/824.html (College application)

**Adult ADHD:**
- http://www.adultadhd.net/ (ADHD in adults)
- http://www.mayoclinic.com/health/adult-adhd/DS01161 (ADHD in adults)
- http://www.webmd.com/add-adhd/guide/adhd-adults (ADHD in adults)

- http://www.additudemag.com/channel/adult-add-adhd/index.html (Career and relationships)
- http://www.mungosadhd.com/ (Great blog and resource)

That's all I got, friends, except for a few parting words of advice: become the expert on and advocate for your own child's treatment. Don't expect or let anyone else take that role for you. Listen to your child. Respect her. Love him. And when it comes time to let them try their wings, stand out of sight below the nest but with a safety net, and don't rush in too soon. What looks like falling may be the most crucial moment in the process of your WonderKid learning to fly.

# ABOUT THE AUTHOR

Pamela Fagan Hutchins lives, loves, laughs, works, and writes in Texas with her husband Eric and their blended family of three dogs, one cat, and the youngest few of their five offspring. She is the award winning author of many books, including *The Clark Kent Chronicles*, *How To Screw Up Your Kids: Blended Families, Blendered Style*, *Love Gone Viral*, *Hot Flashes And Half Ironmans*, and *Puppalicious And Beyond: Life Outside The Center Of The Universe*, and a contributing author to

*Prevent Workplace Harassment* and *Easy To Love But Hard To Raise.*

Pamela is an employment attorney and human resources professional, and the co-founder of a human resources consulting company. She spends her free time hiking, running, bicycling, and enjoying the great outdoors.

For more information, visit **http://pamelahutchins.com**, or email her at **pamela@pamelahutchins.com**. To receive her e-newsletter for announcements about new releases, click on **http://eepurl.com/iITR**.

Skipjack Publishing: **http://SkipJackPublishing.com**

# I AM NOT A WHACKJOB.

I am not some whacko who writes about her labradoodle Schnookums. Let's just get that straight right off the bat. Hell, I'm practically anti-animal, and I don't believe in the Loch Ness Monster, either. Dogs? They shed. Poop. Pee. Barf. Drool. Chew. Bark. Cats? Ditto, except make that yowl instead of bark, plus I'm deathly allergic. That's why currently we have only three dogs and one cat. Oh, and five fish. And I hardly even like them, except for maybe a little. We've cut back, too. It wasn't so long ago the dog count was six, the cat count three, and the fish count innumerable, along with guinea pigs, birds, ducks, rabbits, and a pig. As in swine.

My most vivid memories of growing up in Wyoming and Texas are of animals. We had the normal sorts of pets, plus the absolute luxury of living in the country. I raised sheep for 4-H and rode my horse to sleepovers. We had visitors furry, feathered, and scaly, of both the hooved and clawed varieties. My husband grew up on St. Croix where the animals were different, but his wild upbringing, close to nature, matched mine. His mother tells stories of her sons bringing geckos on the plane from the island to the mainland, and finding their little skeletons outside the family's summer home in Maine months later. Eric's favorite photograph from his youth shows him standing on the beach holding the booby he rescued while surfing, then nursed back to health and released.

As a child, I devoured books about animals, like *Black Beauty* and *Where the Red Fern Grows*. I idolized James Herriot and Jacques Cousteau. I could never quite decide whether to be a veterinarian or a marine biologist or Shamu's trainer. Somehow I sold out early on and became a lawyer, but that didn't stop the animal love. There, I've admitted it: animal love. I ♥ animals, with a big red heart and sparkly glitter. All of them, nearly, except for maybe insects and reptiles. Also I am not a big fan of rats. But other than that, I love every one. Eric and I spend all the time we can outdoors looking for critters, whether we do it from bicycles or cars, or in the water or on our own four feet. We watch *All Creatures Great and Small* on Netflix. Our offspring naturally love God's creatures, too, at least as much as they love their smartphones, and a whole lot more than they love us.

In the Virgin Islands of Eric's youth, Christianity made plenty of room for the ghosts, spirits, and jumbies of obeah, a folk-magic religion with elements of sorcery and voodoo. The locals couldn't comprehend why continentals like me scoffed at what was so plainly true to them, but scoff I did. Ghosts? Jumbies? As in Casper the friendly? It was hard for me to follow — until I met Eric. He and the islands opened my eyes to a world that existed just beyond the visible. Sometimes these non-humans scared me, and sometimes they comforted me. I liked my pets and the animals of the wild better, but I was captivated by the jumbies. Especially the one guarding Annaly, the house we bought in the rainforest.

When my lawyer career morphed into human resources and then I finally started writing, non-humans started spilling out of every story. Sometimes they are the stars, and sometimes they are the supporting actors. No matter their role, they always manage to steal the show from the unsuspecting humans who believe they are the center of the universe.

# FROGGY WENT A'
COURTIN'

All the signs were there. We even talked about them, way back when. "The owners must love frogs," Eric said as we toured the back yard of the house in Houston that would become our home when we left the islands. He nudged a knee-high pottery frog planter with his foot.

"Umm hmmm," I said. I couldn't have cared less. I was calculating our offer.

"That one is odd," he said. He pointed at a large concrete frog Buddha, almost hidden by giant elephant ears and bougainvillea beside the waterfall that poured from the top pond into the middle one. You could see the ponds all the way from the front door, through the seamless full-length back windows. It reminded us of home, of St. Croix in the U.S. Virgin Islands, of our beloved rainforest home Estate Annaly. How could we not buy this house? Eric continued, "It's like a frog shrine."

I remember saying something noncommittal, like, "Whoa, that *is* odd," as I walked back into the house with the real estate agent. In retrospect, she seemed . . . in a hurry.

We moved in on the ninth of March, springtime in Houston. Beautiful springtime. For roughly six weeks, the temperatures are in the seventies and there's a soft breeze. Flowers bloom but mosquitoes don't yet. Sunlight dapples the ground through the vibrant foliage of the trees. Birds don't chirp, they sing. The fragrance is clean, more than sweet. It's heaven. We moved in, and our new house was like heaven.

Until everything arrived from the islands in another month, we had exactly one piece of furniture: a standard double mattress on the master bedroom floor. The kids slept in sleeping bags. It was spare. We ate our meals on paper plates sitting cross-legged on the floor. When we called to each other, our voices bounced from wall to wall in our 4,000-square-foot echo chamber. Still, it was like heaven.

But around midnight during our fateful third week in Houston, the first frog croaked. His piercing rasp drew our attention, but not our consternation. What was one frog to us, here in heaven?

Oh, had it only been one frog. Or one hundred frogs. Or even one thousand. By three a.m., Eric was standing pondside in his skivvies with three hundred pounds of canine looky-loos beside him in the forms of Cowboy the giant yellow Lab, Layla the Gollum-like boxer, and Karma the emotionally fragile German shepherd. I stood in the doorway.

"Fucking frogs," Eric said, no trace of love in his voice.

Well, yes. Yes, they were. Frogs were, ahem, *fornicating* everywhere. It was overwhelming, really. I swear, if you'd Googled "swingers' resort for frogs," you'd get our address. The amorous amphibians held their tongues as soon as Eric switched on the backyard light. Muttering more curses, he snatched them up in stubbornly conjoined pairs and flung them over the fence. I did not dare ask his plan and after ten minutes, I sneaked off to bed.

Night after sleepless spring night, Eric battled the frogs with a homicidal drive. Day after spring day, he shirked his work as a chemical engineer and looked online for ways to off them. This campaign was beginning to drive me insane, too. Their sounds had long since become white noise, or at worst, bedtime music to me. Eric's tossing, turning, cursing, and trips in- and outside, on the other hand, kept me wide awake. He would report the body count when he returned to bed.

"If I could just think of a way to poison them, I could sleep," he said.

"If you poison them, you'll poison the dogs, maybe even birds," I said into my pillow.

"Acceptable collateral damage," he replied.

In response to my urgings for him to quell his frog-blood lust, Eric tried to repatriate his little nemeses. He loaded them into industrial-sized black garbage bags and headed for the bayou. Unfortunately, the good citizens of Houston were on alert for a serial murderer that spring, and a man seen dumping lumpy garbage bags into the waterway attracted attention. Eric had only just barely returned home before the cops came to check him out. Reluctantly, I vouched for him.

The kids got into the spirit. Instead of just one underwear-clad man in the back yard, we now had him (thank the Lord, he'd started taking the time to don a pair of camo shorts—although I had the feeling he'd spring for camo face and body paint, too given the chance) plus the nine-, eleven-, and thirteen-year-old kids. Like me, the dogs were sleeping through most of it now, except when one of the kids would make a particularly good snatch and yell in triumph. At least it was taking care of any lingering need for sex education.

When the children created an offering of dead froggies to the Buddha, I feared the repercussions. And maybe it was my imagination, but I could swear their numbers doubled that night. It was bad. It was very, very bad.

It pains me to admit that I conspired by my silence in the deaths of hundreds of croakers that spring. They died in an endless variety of ways, but mostly Eric heaved them — THUMP, or occasionally SPLAT — against the house. Sometimes he aimed high, and more than once we found dead frogs clear on the other side of the house the next morning, or their desiccated bodies on the roof weeks later.

"Maybe I should have let the cops take you after all," I groused one night as he stomped off. The man seemed by God determined to ensure that I shared his insomnia.

"What?" he said.

"Maybe I should come out and help you after all," I said, and got out of bed. Ugh.

The calendar pages flipped slowly forward. May passed. It wasn't seventy degrees anymore. The flowers wilted and the mosquitoes hatched. A faint smell of decay — mold? — permeated the house, but it smelled no better outside. The sun burned everything in its searing gaze, yet still the frogs croaked out their horny croaks and gamboled nightly in sexual abandon.

"They'll be gone by summer," I said, certain that they would not. That they would never leave. That my husband would be scribbling *REDRUM* across our bathroom mirror by August while the frogs croaked on. Because "frogicide" written backward doesn't spell anything.

And then one day, they stopped. Silence. Sleep. Happiness. Months went by, blissful days leading inevitably toward April. *Make the clock move slower*, I prayed to God.

January. February. March. We hadn't heard them yet, but the little fockers would be here soon. Apri-ri-ri-RIBBITTTTTTT. Eric leaped up in bed as if the frogs were in there with him.

"Honey, stop," I said.

He glared at me. All my man could see was frogs.

I handed him a pair of earplugs that I'd scavenged a few weeks before from his bag of work safety wear. "It's evolutionary, honey, Darwinian. If our species is to survive, we must adapt."

He stared at them, foamy yellow plugs on either end of a neon-orange string. I took his hand, placed them in his palm, and gently closed his fingers around them. I tugged him out of bed and led him out into our humid back yard, picking up a candle and matches on the way. I left the outside lights off and the male frogs sang out in carnal frenzy. I felt primal, like I was entering a hedonist temple.

Before the frog Buddha, I knelt with my husband. I handed him the candle and matches, then nudged him when he didn't respond. "Light it, my love." He did, a penitent virgin on the altar. He lit the candle. "Now, repeat after me," I said.

He mumbled assent and I began. "I, Eric, present myself before you, Buddha of the frogs."

The look he shot me said, "You're out of your flippin' gourd," but I didn't waver, and he repeated my words.

"I promise to do no harm to any of your frog brothers and sisters, henceforth and forevermore."

"I'm not saying that," he said.

"Humor me. We did it your way all last summer," I said. *And honey, I'm voting you off THAT island,* I thought.

He complied with the enthusiasm of Morticia Addams.

"As a token of my sincerity, I pledge to you to wear these earplugs, and to install a frog shrine in our bedroom immediately."

He repeated the oath, then we blew out the candle and tiptoed in perfect solemnity back into our room. There, I pulled two jolly stuffed frogs from a bag and propped them up on a pedestal table by the back window, between Eric and the live frogs.

"You actually went out and bought these in advance?" he asked.

"I knew I had to take matters into my own hands. I love you, and I want our marriage to withstand the test of frogs."

"It's that bad, huh?"

"Oh yeah, it's that bad."

Eric finally — FINALLY — smiled and swatted me on the behind. He put the earplugs in.

"Those are kind of sexy," I said.

"What?" he yelled.

Mission accomplished.